Stop Fighting & Start Talk
Gaining Peace and Perspective On Marriage and Money

Stop Fighting & Start Talking
Gaining Peace and Perspective On Marriage and Money

by
Ed Coambs MBA, MA, CFP®

To My Wife and Son,
You Mean The World To Me

Contents

Part 1 – Beliefs and Spirituality

Chapter

You Are To Grow — 1
Faith Moves Money Decisions — 2
When Making More Money Isn't The Answer — 3
Going Deep With Diver Ed — 4
Limited vs. Unlimited Life: Real Implications — 5
What Are Your True Money Views — 6
3 Reasons To Fear Financial Success — 7
Finding Healing – A Crisis Of Identity — 8
Financial Independence, No Thanks — 9

Part 2 – Feelings and Emotion

Can Money Bring You Happiness — 10
Money Fights, Yes Please — 11
3 Reasons Success Is Elusive — 12
Gratitude Works — 13
Finding Your Financial Voice — 14
Paying Off Credit Cards Sucks — 15
Creating Marital & Financial Security — 16
Who Are You Trying To Please — 17
Money: Nothing But A Number Or Emotions — 18
You Made It! So, What's The Problem — 19

Part 2 – Feelings and Emotion Continued

Living With Too Much Opportunity   20
Eating Out & Loving It   21

Part 3 - Behaviors

It Starts With Me   22
Stop Setting Goals   23
Different Skills Different Places   24
Ordering Your Life   25
Yes We Can Change   26
From Stuck To Un-Stuck   27
Progress Killed At The Expense Of Perfection 28
Overcoming Your Ambivalence   29
Embracing The Relationship Learning Curve   30
Moving Towards Hope   31

Part 4 - Relationships

Creating Financial Success In Your Marriage 32
Explicit & Implicit Money Lessons In Families 33
Friendly Finances   34
Making The Most Of Your Marriage & Money   35
Money Conflict: Getting On The Same Page   36
Why Conflicts Keep Repeating In Marriage   37
Let Go Of Your Agenda
    & Get To Know Your Spouse   38

Part 4 – Relationships Continued

4 Quick Tips To Getting Over
Your Money Arguments 39
Not Just Money: Fears, Feelings &
The Pressure of Marriage 40
How Specialization Gets Us In Trouble 41
Don't Shoot The Messenger 42
Help I Married An Artist 43
Creating Money Harmony, Is It Possible 44

Part 5 – Thoughts and Logic

Creating Vision, Just Like A Polaroid Photo 45
How Automatic Thoughts Get Us In Trouble 46
Trust Is The Key Ingredient To
Financial Success 47
How Money Sayings Get Us In Trouble 48
Where Did All The Money Go? 49
Are You Living The Good Life
& Don't Even Know It? 50
Your Greatest Financial Risk Is Not
What You Think 51

Part 5 – Thoughts and Logic

What Is SMART Money Management   52
Moving Arguments To Resolution   53
8 Tips For Picking A Financial Planner 54

Selected References

Final Thoughts And Connecting

Acknowledgement

Many people have poured into my life. I am grateful to my parents, wife, and son for always believing in me and encouraging me to pursue my dreams. It has certainly come with challenges and setbacks, but knowing I had their love to fall back on allowed me to face my fears and continue forward.

To all my teachers, who have taught me more lessons than I can remember. There is one professor in particular that has really helped shape my thinking about the financial challenges we face in our marriages, and that is Dr. Kelly Breen Boyce of Gordon Conwell Theological Seminary. During my application interview, she asked me "Ed, have you ever considered that the money fights in marriage are a symptom of an underlying issue?" I looked back at her with shock and confusion. At that point, my perspective was permanently shifted. I now see financial challenges as symptomatic of deeper challenges. Thank you, Dr. Breen Boyce. You have helped set the course of my work.

There are also countless books and presentations that I have read and attended along the way. Without the considerable effort of these many people, my thinking would not have advanced to the place that it has. Thank you for your generosity, and this book is building on your work and thought leadership.

Introduction

This book is born out of a desire to help couples navigate and transform they way that they talk about their marriage and money issues. When we get married, we dream of living happily ever after. Yes, even men have a fairy tale hope that their marriage will be the one that ends perfectly. Not long after the wedding vows have been said and the wedding gifts have been put away, the money fights begin. As we all navigate the inevitable hurdles of everyday living and decision making, there are abundant opportunities for conflict regarding the many money decisions that need to be made.

There is no couple that escapes conflicts about money. Whether rich or poor, there are challenges to overcome and grow through. The wise couples learn that money arguments are seldom actually about the money - they are about the variety of thoughts, emotions, behaviors, relational dynamics, and spiritual beliefs we orient our lives around. This book is intended to help couples gain a deeper appreciation of their partner and the range of experiences they have had that drive the way they interact with the family finances. There is not one unique formula that will guide couples through the challenges of talking about money. There is, however, hope that through spending time together and having intentional conversations, that each couple can grow in their love and respect for each other and better appreciate their partner's perspective.

To get the most out of this book, it will be best for both you and your spouse to take one chapter at a time, read it, contemplate, and then respond to the questions and find a time to talk about what you learned.

Spirituality & Beliefs

Chapter 1

You Are To Grow

Despite the chaos of life, I have found that setting aside time every morning for devotions has a calming and centering effect on my day. One piece of scripture continues to move and encourage me and this is why I am compelled to share it in this first chapter. I know not all of my readers are Christians, but I think that there is a powerful message for all of us – regardless of religious affiliation – in the words of 2 Peter 1:5-9 (I'm calling the passage "You are to Grow.") Take a moment to read it and contemplate how it applies to your life.

You are to Grow

2 Peter 1:5-9

For this very reason, make every effort to
Add to your faith, goodness
And to goodness, knowledge
And to knowledge, self control
And to self control, perseverance
And to perseverance, godliness
And to godliness, brotherly kindness
And to brotherly kindness, love.
For if you possess these qualities in increasing
measure,
They will keep you from being ineffective and
unproductive,
In your knowledge of our Lord Jesus Christ.
But if anyone does not have them,
He is nearsighted and blind,
And has forgotten that he has been cleansed from
his past sins.

As I read this short scripture, I am taken aback by the guidance I receive from it. It strikes me that, as I add goodness, knowledge, self-control, perseverance, godliness, brotherly kindness, and love to my faith, I will put myself in a better position to be more effective and productive in my knowledge of God. This passage provides a clear order to specific aspects of life that I can focus on to increase my certainty when it comes to my calling and destiny. Peter is communicating that we are not expected to have each of these attributes perfectly dialed in, but over time, we should focus on growth in all the afore mentioned areas. As a Christian, having a stronger grasp on these qualities will allow me to walk more closely with my Lord and Savior.

Thank you for the opportunity to start this book with something more personal. You will find throughout this book that I often reference personal anecdotes as a way of showing both that growth is possible and that I humbly recognize my own need for continued growth.

I hope that this piece of scripture will increase your faith and affirm that you do not have to have everything together; instead, if you focus on the aforementioned attributes, you will feel yourself walking more confidently in your faith.

Questions For Reflection

What does growth mean for you?

When is a time that you struggled to grow and what did you do to overcome the challenge?

What is the biggest barrier to growth in this season of your life?

Chapter 2

Faith Moves Money Decisions

1. *Your View* - The way that you understand and see God can have a significant impact on your money decisions. For example, if you see God as rich and giving, then do you believe that God should provide for all of your needs and wants, or just the bare necessities? Or maybe you see God as stingy and harsh; does that make you want to hoard all the money you make and have? Reflect on how your view of God influences the way that you interact with money. Perhaps you buy certain things or spend in certain ways to please God. On the other hand, maybe you stay away from things like gambling, drinking, etc. to stay in God's good graces. Who knew your view of God could influence your money decisions?

2. *Your Faith Community* - What has your preacher, pastor, or spiritual leader taught you about money: that you should be giving more or face Hell (a bit extreme in my book)? More likely,

they have taught you to give to the church-building fund, community fund, tithing, world relief organizations, and the list goes on (none of these things are inherently bad). What about your family and friends who go to church; how do they view money as it relates to God? Maybe you always go out to lunch after service. I bet you didn't think about your faith influencing your money decisions that way, did you?

Now, take a few minutes to consider this. Could it be that we don't own anything? God has simply given us a responsibility to be good stewards of what He has provided us. If that is the case, how would you spend your money differently?

Questions For Reflection

1. What is one thing that frustrates you about God and money?

2. What do you believe God says about money?

3. Where has this belief come from and what supports it?

Chapter 3

When Making More Money Isn't the Answer

Who hasn't, at times, felt overwhelmed by the feeling of needing to make more money? I know I have. Even after years of studying personal finance and putting into place practices to define what's enough for my family and I, I still get caught up in the day-to-day grind of feeling like everything would be okay if I just made more money.

However, that's not what your family needs most from you. Rather than money, they really need your presence and engagement. In our fast-paced culture, it is easy to move quickly and not take the time to reflect on our priorities, so let this be one of those moments when you hit the pause button and really look at what is influencing you.

Take some time to answer the following three questions and include the values that they stand for (i.e. Wealth, Family, Compassion, Hard Work, Balance, etc). For example, I love the show Shark

Tank, and if that was all I watched, then I would think life is all about making deals, more money, and creating businesses.

1. Where do you work?

2. Which organizations do you belong to?

3. What type of information (t.v., internet, magazines, and books) do you consume?

Whether intentionally or unintentionally, we consume daily messages from the outside world, through a number of sources, about how to live our lives. There is meaning in all communication, as well as an underlying value. When we become highly attuned to the values of the communication that we are receiving, then we can make conscious decisions about what to do with it.

Recently, I have really enjoyed listening to the business podcast "Entrepreneur on Fire," but after a while, I realized I moved from enjoying and learning valuable insights about the journey of becoming an entrepreneur to being consumed with thinking about how I could grow my business and (as a natural outcome of that) increase my income. While there is a time and place for learning how to grow your personal finances and business, if left unchecked, other priorities and values will get overshadowed, like spending time with family, community events, personal spirituality, etc.

When you start to feel like making more money is the best use of your time, it is time to stop and evaluate the messages you are taking in.

Questions For Reflection

1. What financial views that you hear through work are not in line with your values?

2. What financial views do you hear through the media that are not in line with your values?

3. How do these different views impact the way you manage your finances?

Chapter 4

Going Deep With Diver Ed

On a recent family vacation to Maine, I learned some important lessons about the value of depth. We went on an amazing tour with Diver Ed, and while we stayed in the boat, Diver Ed dove into the cold Atlantic Ocean to share with the tour some of the amazing sea creatures that live below the surface.

Diver Ed is no ordinary diver. He is the most excited and engaging person you could ever want to meet. His passion for getting below the surface of the water and sharing the sea with his tour participants is infectious. For a few moments, I was so excited by his findings that I thought I might want to also put on a dry suit (a special type of wet suit for cold water). Then I reconsidered, as my passion does not lie in the depths of the ocean, but rather in the depths of the soul. There, too, are amazing things to discover. Diving into the soul can be both dangerous and rewarding, but when we come back to the surface after times of reflection, we develop a new appreciation for who we are.

15

Diver Ed talked a lot about how he would find different critters living at different depths. I think this is also true of our soul. As we move deeper into our understanding of our soul, we come to know more of who we are and the complexity of what makes us up. This is why we connect so deeply with incredible artists. They have come to terms with the depths of their soul and express that through their art. The end result is moving and immediately knowable. When we live life from the depths of our soul, we give off a sense of authenticity with which others connect.

Going deep is something that we often fear, but when we have a tour guide like Diver Ed, we can be encouraged to embrace the discovery of who we have been made to become. I personally have been on a transformational journey, and am still on one, in which I am connecting my life with who I have been created to be. A big part of this transformation has been in training to become a counselor at Gordon Conwell Theological Seminary. I have had the chance to explore both psychology and theology. I have examined both what others understand of these subjects and what I understand of these subjects. Additionally, my experiences with a unique and special spiritual program that's directed at attending to the soul have helped me to prune away unnecessary baggage and grow more into the person I have been designed to be.

What I have found to be true is that our familiarity bias, that calls us to leave well enough alone, limits our ability and desire to go deeper. Yet that is the very thing that can pull us out of the situations we find ourselves in and no longer want to be in. Becoming comfortable with soul exploration will have a transformative impact on your life. It will reorient some, if not all, of your goals or reasons for doing things. Life reorientation is a risk we all know intuitively exists and often stops us in the tracks of transformation. The great mystery about soul exploration is that, as you are making new decisions about your life, the old ways no longer seem relevant. Leaving behind what once was important is no longer a big deal.

Let's come back up to the surface of soul exploration. By engaging in soul exploration, you will begin to reorient the way in which you approach life and those matters that cause you the most difficulty. Be it in your marriage, your finances, friendships, or work, as you enter into soul transformation, your perspective and approach begin to shift in ways that allow you to engage life in a more meaningful way.

To go further in your exploration, I recommend checking out Creating a Rule of Life by Steve Macchia.

If you are ever in Bar Harbor, Maine, and you have young children, I highly recommend Diver Ed's Dive-In Theater.

Questions For Reflection

1. What would it feel like to explore your soul?

2. What stops you from exploring your soul?

3. What might be different if you took the time to become reflective?

Chapter 5

Limited vs. Unlimited Life: Real Financial Implications

Recently, I was scrolling through my Facebook newsfeed, and I came across two very different perspectives that got me thinking about how I see the world. The reality is that we all have what is called a worldview - a way in which we order our lives and then make decisions about how to live them. Most of the time, our worldview is socially constructed by years of experiences and observations. We take in a variety of messages, from many different sources, and they all contribute to the way in which we order our days.

So, what did I see on Facebook that got me thinking? Take a minute to read these quotes. How do they sit with you? What do you like about them, and what do you disagree with?

"Life is short. Time is fast. No replay. No rewind. So enjoy every moment as it comes." -- Dr. Meg

Meeker

"Don't let anyone convince you to buy things you don't need. Develop power over purchase and learn to say no." -- Dave Ramsey

In the context of our financial lives, both quotes have very strong messages. The first quote tells me that I should spend whatever money I need to so that I can enjoy the moment. Just yesterday, after lunch with a good friend of mine, I stumbled into a kids' store with my son. I had no intention of buying anything (first mistake right there), yet somehow ended up walking out of the store with $26 worth of toys. Why did I do this? The same reason as any father probably would - because of the momentary joy I got from seeing my sons smiling face with a new dump truck and puzzle. A la the first quote, I was living for the moment.

The second quote evokes another part of me - the financial planner, the one who wants to master money. It reminds me that I should be saving, not spending. It reinforces the idea that, while I do want to experience joy today, I also want to have the resources to be able to enjoy 30 years from now.

Here is the reality, and we all know this, but often lose sight of it: everyday, we are given hundreds (if not thousands) of buying messages and opportunities. While I am a fan of personal responsibility, we must always realize we are working against a strong head wind when it comes to saying no to impulse purchases. We are not absolved of our responsibility for our decision making, but we also must remember that it is a bit more complex than just saying no.

Ultimately, reconciling the desire to enjoy today (i.e. spend) with not buying things you don't need is an ongoing process in the development of my own worldview. As we move through life, we are constantly bombarded with messages about what to think, how to think, and when to think it. The challenge for your financial life is to become increasingly aware of your deepest values and to make decisions from that place. We have to live in the mind frame that we are not guaranteed tomorrow, but there is a pretty good chance that it will come. Finding the balance in your life between joy today and joy many years from now is much more of a fine art than an exact science.

Questions for Reflection

1. On a continuum from live for today and save for tomorrow, where would you place yourself?

2. What circumstances could cause you to move to a different place on the continuum of live for today and save for tomorrow?

3. Where did your messages about live for today or save for tomorrow come from?

Chapter 6

What are Your True Money Views?

What do you really believe to be true about money?

No, really - what do you believe to be true about money? For most of us, we have mixed emotions about the role it plays in our life. Part of learning how to better manage the money and resources we have can come through understanding what we really believe to be true about money. The reality is that some of our beliefs have the potential to limit us and our ability to move to another level of financial peace in our life. While money is not (and should not be) everything in life, it is obviously very important.

To help you clarify your beliefs about money, start by asking yourself, "What do I believe to be true about money?" Then write down every thought that immediately comes into your head. Is it "necessary?" "Inconvenient?" "Fun?" Don't worry about analyzing your ideas too deeply at this moment; just write them down.

Once you are done, look over your notes, and write next to each thought where that particular idea came from. Common sources include family, faith, friends, society, books, and media. The trick is to be as specific as possible.

Now, for everything that you wrote down, try to find at least one exception to that belief. If that's not possible, then you have landed on one of your true money views. The beauty of identifying your true money views is that it gives you freedom in knowing what you believe. When you know what you believe, then you can make forward progress toward creating a deeper sense of financial peace in your life. Every person's concept of financial peace is different, and so the more that you can clearly articulate what is true for you, the less likely you are to feel blown around by the winds of others' views.

One thing to keep in mind as you do this exercise: *true money views change and grow in life.* With each new stage in life, new challenges and opportunities emerge, and what it takes to work through them will change. Remaining flexible will allow you to grow while remaining grounded in what you believe. This will allow you to navigate the inevitable changes in life.

Questions for Reflection

1. What do you believe to be true about money?

2. When have you seen a different view and adapted to it?

3. At what ages have your money views shifted and what prompted the changes?

Chapter 7

3 Reasons Why We Fear Financial Success

Let's face it - our culture is infatuated with success, and not just any ordinary success - wild and crazy financial success. For each person, this may mean something slightly different, but all we have to do is look at the number of television shows that center on large amounts of prize money to be reminded of our preoccupation with cash. I can certainly understand why our culture is obsessed with wealth; we have been taught repeatedly, by media and personal observations, that we do not have enough stuff. So we go off to accumulate more money to get more stuff.

What do you and your spouse believe to be true about financial success? Could your beliefs be preventing you from achieving financial success? How do you define financial success? In the process of defining and reaching for financial success, do you ignore other key areas of your life?

While on the surface, financial success (i.e., having lots of money) seems like it could be great, here are three reasons why we fear it.

1. We won't be able to manage it. With more money comes more responsibility and more ways to manage it. When you are just starting out, all you need is a simple checking account. But as you progress in life, you often get different investment accounts set up. If you really start accumulating more money, there are trusts and different tax structures to consider, and for those who have large sums of cash, they start dealing with multiple businesses, properties, and philanthropies. Progressing up the wealth ladder does not always make life easier; it can actually make things more complex, because there is more to manage.

2. Financial success ruins families. The list of actors, singers, athletes, and lottery winners who have ended up with large amounts of money and then had their family fall apart is too long to detail here. But I will mention one that I remember all too well, and that is MC Hammer. We have also heard countless stories of trust fund kids who have blown their families' wealth. Perhaps you have even met a few rich people and have seen how they struggled to maintain a healthy emotional connection while spending their millions (or billions).

3. **It will create a gap in my spiritual life.** How often have we heard that money is the root of all evil? Well, if that was the case, we would all be in trouble! 1 Tim 6:10 actually says, "For the love of money is a root of all kinds of evil. Some people, eager for money, have wandered from the faith and pierced themselves with many griefs." This is one of over 2,000 Biblical verses that address the management of money and resources. What I have come to understand from my faith is that the raw pursuit of money will end in meaninglessness, frustration, despair, and a separation from God.

So, what are we to do when we fear the implications of living with financial success in our life? Start with the understanding that God owns it all. One example of this comes from Ecclesiastes 5:19: "As for every man to whom God has given riches and wealth, and given him power to eat of it, to receive his heritage and rejoice in his labor-- this is the gift of God." This is one of many verses that refer to God's ownership.

The next step is being aware that financial success has not ruined all families. In reality, there are many families who quietly live with their wealth and merely see it as a tool to facilitate living and being generous with their time and resources. The reason that we do not know about these families is that they don't do anything particularly sensational to put themselves in the public eye. As a result, we miss the opportunity to acknowledge that families can live well with wealth, but it is usually because they have built it up over time and learned how to manage it intentionally. This leads me to my next fear.

While it is true that there is more to manage as you accumulate wealth, there are also skills and relationships that you develop over time as that money comes in. That means that the process of managing the money you have, while certainly still a responsibility, often brings in the necessary skills and relationships to do it well.

The shift in my thinking about financial success centers on significance, which means first recognizing that I don't have to be a millionaire to know that I am richly blessed. More and more, I think less about getting stuff and instead look for opportunities to share my resources and to be a blessing to others.

Questions for Reflection

1. Is financial success achievable?

2. If so, why or why not?

3. What has led you to this conclusion?

4. What would happen to your family if they achieved their own definition of success?

Chapter 8

Finding Healing-- A Crisis of Identity

Wow, October 2013 was an amazing week in Nashville, TN! I was there for the American Association of Christian Counselors (AACC) conference! There were so many great speakers, singers, and most importantly, counselors, pastors, and lay leaders. The energy was contagious and inspiring. It was a great time for learning, growing, sharing, and worshipping.

For all of us at different points in life, we experience pain and tragedy, and yet how we respond to those experiences can have a significant impact on our mental and physical health. Throughout the conference, I got to hear from a wide range of therapists and pastors who approach helping people in many different styles. Despite their differences, there was a resounding theme to the healing process.

35

To find healing, start with your identity, as it can anchor the rest of your healing work. So, where should you anchor your identity? For many of us, we anchor our identity in work, family, possessions, money, drugs, and the list could go on. When we turn to Christ and understand that we are made in the image of God (Gen 1:27), we form an immovable anchor - an anchor based on the Lord's promises to be our provider and sustainer.

However, when we are completely honest, it is hard to own our identity in God, especially when we feel uncertain about who God is. Or, we may flat out refuse to align ourselves with God if we see him as distant, removed, harsh, condemning, or any other host of negative characteristics. Yet when we gain confidence and trust that God is full of love and grace, then we can confidently anchor ourselves in Him. So, it is when we anchor ourselves in Christ that we are ready to begin the journey to restoration.

Questions for Reflection

1. On your journey of spirituality, what role does God play in your life?

2. When have you felt close to God?

3. When have you felt distant from God?

4. What do you anchor your identity in, and why is that important to you?

Chapter 9

Financial Independence, No Thanks!

Our culture tells us that financial independence should be our goal. This idea comes from all the financial institutions and our morals, which promote it. I have recently been watching the show Shark Tank, where this mantra could not be truer, especially for Mr. Wonderful (one of the investors), who says the only important thing in life is making more money.

Yet, when we understand that God owns it all, then we come to realize that we don't ever live in a financially independent state, but rather a financially *inter*dependent state.

Starting with God as the provider, we come to realize that we are in a system where we have to leverage each others' skills and blessings, which places us in a state of interdependence.

39

Recognizing that we live in interdependence can leave us free from the fear of not becoming financially independent. The great thing about financial interdependence is that it does not stop us from pursuing business, but rather, it shifts our focus from looking inward and meeting our own needs to outward and meeting the needs of others.

Ultimately, none of us is free from counting on God or others.

Questions for Reflection

1. How does recognizing that we live in a financially interdependent world change your view of money?

2. Interdependence, at its foundation, requires faith and trust. Where have you been hurt before in this?

3. Do you typically see people as good and trustworthy or unfaithful and hard to trust? How does this impact the way that you manage your finances?

Emotions & Feelings

Chapter 10

Can Money Bring You Happiness?

YES!!!!

This is the good news, according to Catherine Hart Weber. In her recent book *Flourish, Discover Vibrant Living*, she cites the work of researcher Thomas Golovich, who found that, when people spend money on experiences, it creates a lasting positive impact on them. In many cases, that joy increases over time because the memories live on as they are retold among the people who enjoyed the experience together.

Here are five great experience ideas to get you started.

1. Go to your favorite sporting event.
2. Get a massage with someone.
3. Go to the theater and see a play, musical, or concert.
4. Take a trip to the beach with friends.
5. Go to that place you have always wanted.

Questions for Reflection

1. What have been some of your best experiences and the memories that have lived on of them?

2. What experiences have you missed that you are now trying to recreate because you missed them in an earlier part of your life?

3. What experiences do you want to create in the future?

Chapter 11

Money Fights? Yes, Please!

What's that? Did I just encourage you to pick a money fight? No. But when there is a disagreement regarding money in your life, you need to address it and bring it to a resolution. Otherwise, you end up on the merry-go-round of fighting over the same things again and again without reaching resolution. Po Bronson and Ashley Merryman, in their recent book Nurture Shock, expose counterproductive parenting mindsets. In their chapter "Plays Well With Others," they dig into the research regarding arguments in the home and the impact they have on the couple as well as on the children. What they found from the work of Dr. E. Mark Cummings, at the University of Notre Dame, is that, despite the popular notion that parents fighting in front of children is detrimental to the child's well being, in reality, it can be beneficial for them.

Let me explain. Based on Cummings' work, he has found that children are "emotional Geiger-counters," so even with the parents' best attempts to avoid conflict in front of their children, the kids are still aware something is going on, even if they don't know the nature of it. Even more detrimental to children is watching their parents start a fight and then taking it to another room to attempt to resolve it in private. When this happens, the kids miss an important opportunity to see proper modeling of conflicts being squashed. That process actually "improves their sense of security, over time, and increases their prosocial behavior at school, as rated by teachers" (Bronson & Merryman, pg. 185).

Questions for Reflection

1. What would create a safe place to fight?

2. What topics are permissible to fight about in front of your kids?

3. What would you like your kids to know about fighting?

Chapter 12

3 Reasons why Success is Elusive

Let's face it; we are a culture infatuated with success. From the shows on TV, to magazines in stores, and the countless blogs dedicated to the subject, success is deeply ingrained in our culture. Yet when I ask people about success, many don't feel like they have reached it yet. Why is this? Here are three reasons why so many of us feel like success is elusive.

1. You and your spouse have a different idea about what success looks like.

2. You change your mind about what success looks like.

3. You have had some successes, but shortly thereafter, the goal increases. Then you achieve that bigger goal, and again the goal becomes bigger, and the cycle continues this way, leaving you chasing that feeling of success.

So success is getting 80% of the way there, because by the time you get to that point, you are likely starting to set up your next target. This is why life becomes a series of progressive successes. The important thing to remember as you move through life is to enjoy the peaks of success, but not to despair when you cross over the peak and are back down in the valley. Just look up again to where you are headed. Success is not done until you stop looking up the mountain for the next opportunity.

With this in mind, now think about your financial life. Would a 20 year old you look at the 30 year old you and say "WOW, you are successful?" Would the 30 year old you look at the 50 year old you and say "Wow, you are successful?" Hopefully.

The problem for most of us is that we quickly forget that are former successes are now just our normal. As a teenager, you dreamed of having a car, and now you take it for granted. As a young adult, you dreamed of buying a home, and now you want the new, larger home. Coming out of college you just wanted to land a job, and now you want to get the six figure job. The list could go on in this fashion.

My question to you is, are you successful? My answer is, I am.

Don't stop reaching for new heights, but recognize that you are successful.

Questions for Reflection

1. What successes have you forgotten about that you need to remember when you feel unsuccessful?

2. Who defines success for you?

3. When is it time to stop pursuing success in one area of life so that you can have success in another?

Chapter 13

Gratitude Works

Gratitude has the power to heal, energize, and change lives. I recently heard a presentation by Dr. Robert Emmons of UC Davis, who researches the impact of gratitude on people's lives. I was taken aback by the impact of gratitude. Did you know that based on Dr. Emmons findings, people who regularly practice an attitude of gratitude have on average a 7% higher income then those people who don't?

To develop gratitude in your life, Dr. Emmons recommended starting a gratitude journal. He gave three simple steps to increasing the effectiveness of your gratitude journaling.

1. Specificity - be specific about what you are grateful for.
2. Surprise - write about something you received unexpectedly. (Anything from a compliment to a large gift.)
3. Scarcity - wanting now what you may not have later. (Imagine having no money. Now, how grateful are you for the money that you have?)

My guess is that we can all increase our level of gratitude and decrease our frustrations with our spouses and financial situations when we start to focus more of our energy on gratitude.

I am grateful for a lot of things, but one of my favorites right now is my son's laughter at the simple things in life. He is two and half years old and finds the simplest things so delightful. Just the prospect of going swimming will have him jumping up and down for joy. His simple pleasures remind me not to take life too seriously and to have fun.

Questions for Reflection

1.What are you grateful for?

2. How often do you feel grateful and what creates that experience for you?

3. How often do you share your gratitude and what would it take to increase your level of sharing?

Chapter 14

Finding Your Financial Voice

There are more personal finance gurus out there than you can shake a stick at. How do you know who to trust and what advice to integrate into your life? There are so many questions when considering the variety of financial tips and tricks that are available.

But the real challenge is to find your own financial voice. What do you believe to be true about the value of money? Is this something you share or keep to yourself? Knowing yourself – spiritually, mentally, emotionally, – is one of the most important parts of the human journey. I ask you to know yourself *financially* as well. Define for yourself what you believe to be true about money. Stop looking at external influences for a moment and spend some time writing down all that you believe to be true about money.

Understanding our thoughts, beliefs, and feelings will be helpful in creating the financial life that we want, but it's important to note that some of your views will be limiting. The challenge is to separate which ones to keep and which ones should go. However, you won't know how to proceed until you have taken the time to know what you think, believe, and feel about money.

Try this simple exercise. Look at each word below, and write down the first feelings/ideas that come to mind next to them.

Money:

Wealth:

Poverty:

Investing:

Debt:

Now that you have taken action, continue with other money- related words that stimulate strong responses for you, and write down your first thoughts to those as well.

If you really want to step up your growth, share this with your spouse and ask if he or she would be willing to do the same with you. You will be amazed at what you learn about how your partner sees money.

Questions for Reflection

1. What surprised you most about the above exercise?

2. What views do you feel like you need to change?

3. How would changing those views impact your life?

Chapter 15

Paying Off Credit Cards Sucks

I was recently reminded of a dirty little secret: Crushing credit card debt is not just for the low-income or average-income family. It also hits families making great money too.

I was working from Panera recently and happened to meet a man who was there to pick up the day-old bagels for delivery to local homeless shelters. When we got to talking, he shared with me that he works for a credit counseling agency in the area. Since I am always trying to make better sense of the actual financial lives people live, I asked him who his clients were. Boy was I surprised when he said they included members of that country club up the road. As we talked a bit more, he revealed that all it takes is one job loss for people to get into deep trouble with their debt.

The reason this conversation surprised me was that I assumed that, if you can afford to be a member of an exclusive environment like a country club, then you probably have plenty of money in the bank to cover your expenses for years to come. But this is not always the case; for all of us, debt represents a promise to pay for something we buy today with money we will earn in the future. This thinking works great until our ability to earn that money changes for a wide variety of reasons.

So, why does paying off credit cards suck? Because it means that we have to pay for our past when we would rather just move on. The reality, though, is that we must address what has happened in the past before we move into the future with our finances. Otherwise, our debt will continue to serve as an anchor to the future growth of our finances.

To attack debt, you must come at it from two angles: logical and emotional.

Logical:
1. List all of your debts together on one page (include balance, interest rate, minimum payment, credit card company name, and phone number.)

2. Organize what you owe from smallest to highest amount.

3. Call each of the credit card companies to negotiate a lower interest rate.

4. Work out a debt snowball plan. Dave Ramsey lays this out in an easy-to-understand way.

Emotional:
1. Reflect on what was going on in your life that caused you to spend so much on credit cards. It may have been a stressful season, or perhaps you were counting on a pay raise that never came.

2. Were you buying out of guilt, fear, anxiety, etc.? It's important to acknowledge the root of your spending to learn how to get your situation under control.

3. Think about where you get your true sense of meaning in life. Is it from consumption of goods and services, or is there something else that can help give you meaning that will not cause you to spend beyond your income?

At the end of the day, being in credit card debt does not make you a bad person. Too often, I see people beat themselves up for the situation in which they've ended up. Often, however, the reasons why people have ended up in credit card debt are vast and complex; no two cases are alike. It is more important to take a stand and realize that there is hope in what may feel like a hopeless situation. The first step is acknowledging that you need help.

Questions for Reflection

1. What do you tell yourself about debt?

2. What does debt represent to you?

3. When have you seen debt used wisely, and how does this influence you now?

4. When have you seen debt abused and how does this influence you now?

Chapter 16

Creating Marital and Financial Security

We want what we want, and we want it now. It has been said time and again that patience is a virtue, but who has that virtue? In reality, many people do, but they are often living quiet and unassuming lives. They have not garnered great community awareness or media attention, yet they are still making a difference in the world in which they live.

Great patience and perseverance are often the keys to building a strong marriage and financial relationship. When couples allow one good gesture or decision to build onto another, it starts the compounding effect. A great example of this is setting money aside towards retirement. The early decision to do so will be challenging and it will feel like not much is happening, but it is, and over years and decades you will recognize the difference the concerted effort is making. You will also see the difference when you have friends who made the decision to live for today and then, as they approach retirement, do not have the necessary resources to pursue or maintain the life style they have grown accustomed to.

So, what stops us from moving forward? Too often, it comes out of the fear that there will not be enough resources at the next step or stage of life, that somehow love and money are zero-sum items, and that once you consume them, there will be no more. Yet, when we realize that both love and money are currencies that can be exchanged over and over again, our fear of running out can melt away.

Moving from impulsivity to patience and perseverance creates opportunities for our decisions to become intentional and to build on each other. But when we jump from one method to another without giving things a chance to work, we miss the opportunities to witness growth. This happens all the time while saving for retirement. We get distracted when we hear or read about a hot tip and we think we should follow it, but the reality is that having a strong plan that you consistently stick with is going to be far more valuable than any one hot investment that will save the day. Sure, we would all love every decision to grow without setbacks, but this is not reality.

None of us is born with all the requirements to form a great marriage or achieve financial security. Fortunately though, experience, learning, mentorship, and a host of other factors are great opportunities for both of these experiences to happen.

So, what is the compounding effect? It is a realization that early, good decisions often do not show great results, but continued good decisions show tremendous results.

Let's take a look at an example of how a great marriage emerges. It starts long before two people ever meet; in reality, it begins at conception. During childhood, we are exposed to a wide variety of experiences, many of which are the building blocks that form our future relationships. Once we reach dating age, we continue in our growth and learning about relationship dynamics. At some point, one of those relationships leads to marriage, and this is where things start to get really interesting. In a new marriage, couples start to form the shared understandings that will define their relationship, and those experiences in the first years set the course for what life will continue to look like. By ten years into marriage, the couple will certainly have had some challenges along the way, but if they have remained committed to growth and support, then their feelings of commitment and love can grow deeper than they ever imagined. As the years continue to progress, it is possible that the bond between the couple will continue to grow. After 40 to 50 years of marriage, the couple will have adult children, grandkids, and perhaps great grandkids, who look at their marriage and are amazed by the love they have for each other. But to get to this place, it took the compounding effect: a "building-upon" of many experiences together, both good and bad.

The same is true for building financial security and abundance in your life. No one is born with all the knowledge they need to create financial security for themselves. They must remain on a continuous learning path to ensure that they can navigate each stage of life. The skills needed in your early twenties are not the same as those needed in your forties, and they are certainly not what are needed in your sixties and beyond.

The challenge for both building a great marriage and creating financial security is a long-term perspective. It takes an ability to look out ahead 20, 30, and 40 years and have a vision for where you want your life to end up. While no one can be a fortune teller and know the future, they can have a view of what they would like their life to look like.

No matter where you are in your journey of marriage and money management, there are abundant resources to help you grow. Here are two books I recommend to help you on your journey.

Love Sense by Dr. Sue Johnson

Mind Over Money by Dr. Brad Klontz & Dr. Ted Klontz

Questions for Reflection

1. What are the decisions, actions, and thoughts that lead to a powerful marriage?

2. What are the decisions, actions, and thoughts that lead to a strong financial life?

3. What is compounding in your favor right now?

Chapter 17

Who Are You Trying To Please?

Trying to get the right answers to complex problems can be a daunting task. In the world of marriage and money, there are so many different points of view and perspectives on building and maintaining security that it is easy to become overwhelmed, frustrated, and disillusioned. In *Book Yourself Solid*, author Michael Port shares a short and fun fable that we can all relate to.

The Old Man, the Boy, and the Donkey

An old man, a boy, and a donkey were going to town. The boy rode on the donkey and the old man walked beside him. As they went along, they passed some people who remarked it as a shame the old man was walking and the boy was riding. The man and boy thought maybe the critics were right, so they changed positions.

Later, they passed some people who remarked, "What a shame! He makes that little boy walk."

They then decided they both would walk.

Soon they passed some more people who thought they were stupid to walk when they had a decent donkey to ride. So they both rode the donkey.

Later, they passed some people who shamed them by saying how awful to put such a load on a poor donkey. The boy and man said they were probably right, so they decided to carry the donkey. As they crossed the bridge, they lost their grip on the animal, and he fell into the river and drowned.

The moral of the story? **If you try to please everyone, you might as well kiss your ass goodbye.**

How telling, right? In this story, the man and the boy are both trying to please each new idea that comes their way, and in the end, they lose the donkey that would have carried them into town.

The same is true in the pursuit of trying to master marriage and money. Each author, t.v. pundit, blogger, pastor, family member, and friend is going to have a different perspective on how you should ride your donkey to your destination. The challenge is to have enough confidence in your ability to make decisions that are right for you and your family and to stick with them.

Take time to really consider who you are listening to and what influence they are having on your ability to lead your family. There is a place and a time to challenge your understandings, but there is also a time to rest and enjoy the sweet season of life you are in. Allow yourself to turn off the different voices and enjoy silence on the subject of marriage and money.

Questions for Reflection

1. Who do you try to please?

2. Why?

3. What happens if you shut that influence out?

Chapter 18

Money: Nothing But a Number or Nothing But Emotions

To say that my wife and I respond to and see numbers differently would be an understatement. Okay, okay - I know there isn't a couple who hasn't had an argument about finances in their marriage. But how many couples feel like they understand why they get into so many of the same arguments?

Recently, I shared with my wife, just before she walked out the door for work, that we needed a certain amount of money to cover some upcoming bills. When she got home that evening, she told me that she worried all day about it. I was surprised, because I thought what I shared was objective, but in reality, it was interpreted as us not having enough to pay our bills – which wasn't the case at all.

But wait - numbers are objective, right? I mean, what do you think when you read the word "two?" The number, I would imagine. But what happens when I add more context and write "$2?" Suddenly, the meaning changes.

Numbers, in and of themselves, are objective pieces of data, but what they represent can be very emotional. That is why you can have two people look at the same budget, financial goal, or investment and feel very different about it.

Bottom line: it is important to take time to slow down and understand what the numbers represent to your spouse and how they are interpreting them.

Sure, it would be nice if we all saw the situation objectively, but that's not always the case. For example, if I typed "$1,000," what would you think? Now, what if I added that that's what I brought in for the week?

Talking about money from an emotional perspective can be both exciting and refreshing when we keep a few simple tips in mind.

1. **Time it** - If you regularly get into fights about a household finance topic, set aside a specific time to address it.

2. **Explore it** – Ask your significant other, "What does this information mean to you? How does this information impact you?"

3. **Define** it - Create shared definitions of what it means to budget, invest, save, to have money, to not have money, and any other terms where you typically got stuck.

4. **Delve into your family history** - Learn about how money was used in your spouse's family of origin. Ask how their Mom or Dad viewed and talked about finances.

5. **Exercise patience and persistence** - Remember that talking about money can be hard, and you will not always agree. Be willing to stick it out and learn more about your spouse.

Questions for Reflection

1. What financial conversations bring up the most strife in your marriage?

2. Do you define the problem as logical or emotional?

3. What are 5 potential reasons why your spouse defines it differently than you?

Chapter 19

You Made It! So, What's the Problem?

Here is the reality: managing personal finance is a skill. Nobody is born with the magical gene of good financial management. Just like you didn't become a rock star at your work overnight, you cannot expect to become an expert at managing and talking about your finances in the blink of an eye. Over time, and with some vulnerability, you can start to develop the skills necessary to feel like you have control over your finances.

The good news is you're successful and highly talented. The bad news is that those skills don't necessarily translate into being a personal finance master. So, if you are feeling frustrated that you are making more money than you imagined but continue to struggle financially, you are not alone. The problem is that most of us are too embarrassed to talk about it.

We want to appear as if we have it all together. It is frustrating when money is one of the most talked about subjects in the media and yet, in our personal lives, we still feel lost on how to actually manage our household finances. We feel uncertain about what to believe and how much time we should put into managing the household finances. When we don't see eye-to-eye with our spouses about money, it is sometimes easier to just throw up our hands and say, "I quit. I will just go make more money to solve this problem."

So, if you are making more money than you ever imagined and still feel broke, take a risk and ask for help. Asking a trained Certified Financial Planner, who will not judge you for your current situation and will offer advice and guidance, can become a powerful step toward getting control over your money.

Questions for Reflection

1. What does it mean to you to ask for help?

2. When has asking for help in the past helped you and how did it help you?

3. What are you afraid of revealing in the process of asking for help?

Chapter 20

Living With Too Much Opportunity

The reason we struggle financially is that we have too much opportunity. That's right – *too much opportunity*. How on Earth is that even possible?

You may feel like you need more money so that you can go on the vacation you have always dreamed of, start saving for retirement, buy a new car, redecorate the house, and the list goes on. And that is my very point: because there are so many different ways to spend your money, having a myriad of choices can often feel overwhelming, and it feels as if you do not have enough to make it all possible.

So, how did we get here? Remember the good old days, back in college, when you had limited funds and were excited just to go out and get a few beers with friends? Now you have moved on, had several pay raises, and you are making more money. You went from only being able to afford the cheapest, most watered-down beverage to becoming a beer connoisseur. There are more options out there than you ever imagined. Who would have thought?

Ok, so maybe beer isn't your thing; perhaps it is travel. In the cash-strapped days of college, you loved road trips with your friends. You would cram into the car, drive to the beach, and find the cheapest hotel you could stand. But not now. These days, you take a road trip with your family, and you are looking for the Holiday Inn, or perhaps you skip driving to the local beach and instead head to a beautiful island destination. Again, you start to realize there are always "better" opportunities out there.

As we continue to make more money, we learn to see new opportunities that we never knew existed. But we don't stop there -- we pursue them. Eventually, we're introduced to even more opportunities. This is what makes life exciting, fun, and somehow totally overwhelming.

There is always more, but it comes at a cost when we don't add balance and satisfaction into our life. I know very happy and very disillusioned people who have plenty of money to pursue a wide range of opportunities, yet that's not what makes them happy. Rather, it's the way they have managed their expectations about what life is really all about.

Use these 5 questions to help you reflect on your feelings about opportunity.

1. What do you remember from the days when you had limited resources?

2. What makes you feel like you will never have enough money?

3. Do you feel disappointed if you can't purse the newest opportunity?

4. When do you get overwhelmed by the number of directions in which you feel pulled in your life?

5. How satisfied are you immediately after pursuing a new opportunity? Rate this on a scale of 1 to 10 and then examine 5 different new opportunities. Is there a trend? If so, this can be guidance for which opportunities to pursue.

Up to this point, we have just thought about your

opportunities. Let's add in your spouse; how many different opportunities do they have? Managing them becomes one of the biggest challenges in marriage, as now there are your opportunities, your partner's opportunities, and your opportunities together. Oh, wait, but there is more (sorry, just had to say it): you add kids into the mix, and the number of opportunities now looks like some sort of unsolvable calculus equation.

Here are three steps intended to help you tame your family's opportunities and gain a sense of peace again.*

1. Write the name of each family member down.

2. In a second column, have each family member write down all the different opportunities they want to pursue.

3. Have each member prioritize their opportunities. Each person then picks two to work toward.

This is not to say there won't be a time for other opportunities; it is just an exercise to set a direction for the time being.

Chapter 21

Eating Out And Loving It

Okay, okay - I know every financial planner tells you that you should not eat out too much, that you should be saving that money for your future. So why is it so hard to stop going out to eat? What is it about the experience that makes us choose it over putting aside what we end up spending on a meal? I have identified five very beneficial reasons that families continue to go out to eat and love it.

1. It's a social experience that gives you the opportunity to relax and enjoy the company of your family. Sometimes you get the added pleasure of bumping into friends at your favorite restaurant, which adds to the whole ambiance.

2. Going out to eat relieves four points of stress: planning a meal, picking up the ingredients, preparing the food, and cleaning up after cooking. Let's face it, when you dine out, all you have to do is pick something off the menu, and someone handles the rest.

3. That leads me to my third point: It also allows us to feel cared for. There is nothing better than going to your favorite restaurant and having someone else take care of you. Many of us spend our days focused on the needs of others – whether at work or at home – and, at the end of the day, it is just so pleasurable to have someone do something for you.

4. Dining out adds variety and diversity to our eating routines. Pleasing everyone in the family is difficult, and at least when you go to a restaurant, there is a variety of options. Each family member can pick what they like and can skip "Mom's meatloaf" for one evening.

5. Most families are consumed with more activities than time to accomplish them all. Eating out leaves families with more time to spend at work, or attend to kids, or travel to and from activities.

So, when it comes to dining out, how can you eat your cake and have it too? Take these three baby steps.

1. Try to determine how much you need to retire. Here is a link to a simple calculator to get you started.

2. Set a goal for how much money you can save for the future every month and have it automatically drafted out of your bank account into an IRA account.

3. If you are not able to give up going out to eat, consider eating at more affordable places, or sign up for services like Living Social or Groupon that offer coupons for local restaurants. Keep an eye out for dining specials on social media like Yelp and Foursquare, too. After all, every bit helps!

Questions for Reflection

1. What is your favorite dining out experience?

2. What is a restaurant you have dreamed of eating at but have not tried? Why?

3. If you could eat a meal with anyone, who would it be and what would you ask them?

Behavioral

Chapter 22

It Starts with Me

One of the deepest questions we tend to ask ourselves is, "Am I acceptable?" How we go about finding the answer varies widely.

When it comes to knowing if we are making the right decisions in our marriage and with money, there are a proliferation of books, articles, and thought leaders all willing to divulge the "right way" to do it (I am one of them). Yet, when you spend too much time consulting these sources, it doesn't take long to feel completely overwhelmed by the various views and approaches they offer. When we only look outside ourselves for the answer to whether we're acceptable, then we are relying on external validation to give our lives meaning.

We all do it. That's because external validation allows us to compare and contrast the life that we are living to the lives of others. Let's face it - no matter how hard we try not to think about the Joneses, at some point, we inevitably examine how our life stacks up to other people's, as this gives us opportunities to see where we can grow. Yet the challenge that this creates is that we can be left feeling inadequate and unacceptable if external validation is our only source of self-worth.

Let me share an example to make my point. I have read countless books on the topic of personal finance. I love the subject, yet the more I read, the more I have come to realize that I cannot possibly embrace all of the different views of "financial success." Why? When I think about the myriad of advice and offerings about money, I see a continuum of beliefs about what financial success looks like. Some people see it as having the most money, while others say it's living a simple life without material things. So, given the spectrum of opinions, what am I to do if I want to live a financially successful life?

It starts with me. Instead of confusing myself even more by trying to process everyone else's opinion, I will use internal validation to decide what financial success looks like for me. Internal validation starts with saying that I am acceptable no matter where I am in my life. It acknowledges that I have the potential for growth and change, all the while maintaining my acceptability. Internal validation is what we use to help measure which sources of external validation we want to integrate into our life and which sources we want to leave out. It says I have the ability to make my own decisions about what is right for my life, and I don't have to become what others tell me to become. When we develop a strong sense of internal validation, then we can answer the question, "Am I acceptable?" with a resounding "YES!"

Questions for Reflection

1. Are you acceptable?

2. When do you feel most unacceptable?

3. What helps you feel acceptable?

Chapter 23

Stop setting goals

What happens to you when you hear the word "goal?" For some, it generates excitement. Others, however, shut down. Everyone has a philosophy on goals; what is yours?

After reading a recent blog post titled "Stop Setting Goals" by Gene Hamilton, I started thinking about my own philosophy on goals. In a nutshell, Gene recounts his desire to become a top mountain biker, but when he finally accomplishes his goal, he feels empty rather than fulfilled. Why? Because he focused so hard on pursuing his dream that he ended up neglecting (and losing) a great girlfriend, friends, family, and a home. Years later, he decided to take another stab at being a top mountain biker, but this time - while his ultimate goal hadn't changed - he focused on experiencing success daily by acknowledging small milestones along the way and trusting that they would lead to his ultimate goal. For Gene, the small milestones included interval training, hill climbs, and distance days, and at the end of each of them, he would celebrate his accomplishment. What happened the second time around? Sure enough, Gene enjoyed accomplishing both his smaller goals and the big one of being a top-ranked mountain biker.

How can this lesson help us on our journey toward financial success? Maybe an example might help. Let's say that your goal is to have a million dollars, but you have not yet started working on getting there. You can break down this goal into many, many small parts that can be celebrated along the way (just like Gene). Step one might look like opening a savings account, step two would be to set up an automatic payment of $10 a week to that account, step three would be to read a book about investing, step four is to be determined...Once you figure out what the big goal is and break it down into the smaller pieces, forget about the larger picture and just focus on living out the smaller, timelier successes. The big goal will then naturally follow the regular attainment of the smaller goals.

Questions for Reflection

1. When has goal setting help you?

2. What goal of yours can you break down into smaller pieces?

3. What are the smaller pieces of the bigger goal? Define 3 or 4 pieces of the bigger goal and then leave the rest to be determined after completing the first smaller goals.

Chapter 24

Different Skills Different Places

You are an amazing lawyer, doctor, accountant, business person, radio personality, you name it. Whatever your occupation, let's assume that you see yourself as great at what you do; you've achieved fantastic results, been rewarded with bonuses and promotions, and every year, you have more responsibilities and challenges ahead of you. Maybe you've thought along the way, "If I just get to this next level, my life will be easier," but so far, you have not seen that to be the case.

Our work, whether we like it or not, hugely influences the way we see ourselves, as well as many other aspects of our life, including family. Yet I have noticed time and time again instances where the qualities that make us successful at work actually impede our ability to flourish at home. For example, I have been training to become a marriage counselor, and just last night my wife and I talked about how I have become a better listener, which is required for the job. At

104

the same time, I often get frustrated in personal relationships because it feels like no one asks about me. My loving wife made the observation that perhaps it is because I am too busy asking questions and trying to understand everyone else that I don't give others the chance to know me.

So, I ask you to examine and define for yourself what it means to achieve results in your career and with your family. To get the ball rolling, here are three simple but profound questions to ask yourself. After answering the following about yourself, ask your spouse to do the same thing for you, then challenge them to answer these questions for themselves as well.

1.   Which skills and attributes make me great at my job?

2.   Which of my skills and attributes will help my family flourish?

3.   With answers to the two previous questions in mind, which skills and attributes do I need to leave at the office?

The lesson is that there can be overlap in the skills

and attributes that are needed for work and home life, but not all will transfer. When we see this clearly, then both our work and home life have a stronger chance of flourishing.

A fun way to clarify the picture of what is good for work and home is to use a Venn diagram. Using a Venn diagram to organize what is best for work and home will clarify where there are differences and where there is overlap in the skills and attributes you bring home to your family. Title one circle work, the other home. Fill in the circles with the skills and attributes that support work and home life. Then look for the overlaps and fill in the middle overlapping part of the circles.

Questions for Reflection

1. What challenged you about this exercise?

2. What did you learn from the exercise?

3. What will you start to do differently based on the exercise?

Chapter 25

Ordering Your Life

What is important in your life? Kids, marriage, God, work, friends, yourself, family... How important are each of these to you? Stop. Take a minute to get out a piece of paper and write them in your order of priority. When you take time to intentionally rank these aspects of your life, you then have a guideline for making decisions. If it comes down to spending time with your spouse or working longer on that work project, it will now be easier to make the decision based on your list.To get a clear and bold picture of how you *really* order these aspects of your life, email ten of your closest friends and family members, and ask them for their candid feedback on how THEY think you'd order them.

Sample email:Hi, friends and family -   I am trying to grow in my personal awareness and improve my sense of priority. Would you please take a minute to help me?   I know how I think I order these different aspects of my life. What I would like to know is how YOU think I do: Friends, Marriage, Kids, Work, God, Myself, and Family.

Please feel free to include any feedback about why you ranked them in the order that you did.

Your feedback will help me identify my blind spots and continue to grow intentionally.

Questions for Reflection

1. How did you order kids, marriage, God, work, friends, yourself, family?

2. Is your ordering the ideal or reality?

3. Did you take the risk of emailing friends and family? What was that like?

Chapter 26

Spend A $100 Or I Will Be Mad At You

Celebrations of birthdays, babies, weddings, and holidays always come with great expectations - especially when it comes to our money. Even when the invitation says "no gifts," there's always pressure to spend. Recently, I was in a coffee shop and I overheard a woman telling a friend over the phone about how her family was going to get mad at her if she didn't spend a hundred dollars on a gift for an upcoming celebration.

Her dilemma raises an interesting question about what to do when someone threatens you with a strong emotion when you don't want to do something. This is where having a healthy sense of boundaries and ownership of emotions can be really beneficial. The reason that people use strong emotions to evoke you into doing something is that they know that it works on you. But when you choose to react differently and let that person own their emotions, then you are free to respond in a way that is congruent with your values.

So, what does this look like in practical terms? Let's try seeing it through the lens of a hypothetical conversation between our coffee shop friend and her relative.

Family Member: You need to buy Sally a $100 gift for her birthday or I will be so mad at you.

Coffee Shop Woman: You are entitled to your feelings, and I respect that. But I have made the decision to do something different this year.

Family Member: I can't believe you. I am so mad! How can you not buy this gift for Sally?

Coffee Shop Woman: Please know that I love Sally very much, and I am happy to come to her party if you would still like me there.

In their book *Boundaries,* Doctors Cloud and Townsend provide many great guidelines about establishing and maintaining healthy boundaries. They also address eight common myths about setting them. In the case of our coffee shop friend,

I think myth number eight is particularly important.

Myth #8: Boundaries are permanent and I'm afraid of burning my bridges.

While the coffee shop woman is saying no to buying a $100 gift for Sally this time, she is not saying no forever. Rather, she is just saying that, right now, it does not make sense for her to purchase the gift. The important thing to remember is that she does not have to justify her reason for making the decision, but rather, she can just own the fact that she has the right to make her own choices about what to do with her money.

Questions for Reflection

1. What is your reaction to the coffee shop woman? Why?

2. Who do you need to set firmer boundaries with?

3. Who do you need to open your boundaries with?

Chapter 27

From Stuck to Un-Stuck

When we get stuck trying to solve a financial problem, what do we do? Google. That's right - Google has all the answers we need at our finger tips. With one good search, we can answer and solve any problem: budgeting, investing, saving, couponing, starting a business, you name it.

Our thinking goes that if we can just find the right information about managing money, then we will not be financially stuck anymore.

But is this reality? No. Absolutely not.

Information alone often does not move people from a place of feeling stuck. Addressing feelings, beliefs, and relationship dynamics, then taking action - that's what gets people un-stuck.

We all experience negative feelings about money, organizing, investing, profit, math, the economy, etc. that are old and well-ingrained (from our family, friends, and spiritual life) from time to time. We also have subconscious fight-flight

115

reactions that interfere with our ability to take in financial information and integrate it in a way that matches what we believe.

Moving from "stuck" to "unstuck" takes intention. There are three important questions to ask yourself to get you rolling again.

1. What do I believe to be true about whatever financial topic has me stuck?

2. Where did this belief come from?

3. What purpose does this belief serve, and how does it limit my ability to live in a way that I desire?

Moving from stuck to un-stuck is a process. Asking questions of yourself can help identify your sticking points. If you really are stuck and can't make progress on your own, then it is time to call in the help of an expert. Appropriate experts might include either a Certified Financial Planner or Counselor.

Questions for Reflection

1. Where do you feel stuck in your finances or marriage?

2. What story do you tell to explain this position?

3. How does this story maintain the very thing you are trying to move through?

Chapter 28

Progress Killed At The Expense Of Perfection

True confession, there is no perfect financial plan. Whew, there, I said it. As a financial planner, I would love to think that I could craft a bullet proof, perfect financial plan. The reality is that our lives are complex and dynamic, with many changing variables. When we come to terms with this reality, then we will not allow perfection to stop progress towards our financial goals.

The reality is that as we move through our life, our goals grow and change. Think back to the days when you where in college and all you could think about was just getting out of school and getting a job. Now perhaps you are married, have several kids, a house, a job, and who knows what else? Have your goals and plans changed and evolved? More than likely. So what's stopping you now from just taking some steps towards your financial plan? The reality is that until you start moving towards your financial plan, you will not know how you need to adjust it.

Yet many people become paralyzed in committing to a plan for the future because they fear that either they won't achieve the plan or that it is the wrong plan. Don't let either of these fears stop you from creating and implementing a financial plan. Your financial plan should not be written in stone, but rather electronically, so that it can be easily updated as you make new decisions.

Ultimately, your plan will need updating. That is the one thing you can plan on.

Questions for Reflection

1. What keeps you from moving forward with your financial plan?

2. By having a financial plan, what would have to change?

3. How do you think that having a financial plan will change your life?

Chapter 29

Overcoming Your Ambivalence

Are you at a point in your life where you know you need to move forward but you feel stuck? You know that moving forward has the possibility of upsetting the apple cart, so you stay where you are instead of moving forward towards your goal. Often times, we know we need to move forward, but we don't. Why is that? Because beyond knowing all the reasons we are supposed to change, we are also influenced by our emotions, behaviors, and relational dynamics. Anytime we are attempting a significant change, it involves what we know, we believe, we feel, and the way we interact.

In order to move through your ambivalence and towards change, here are six questions to ask yourself. If you can have someone else ask you these questions, this experience will be even more powerful. Take a risk and try it.

1. Why would you want to make this change?

2. How might you go about it in order to succeed?
3. What are the 3 best reasons for you to do it?
4. How important is it for you to make this change and why?
5. So what do you think you'll do?
6. How will your relationships change?

The goal is ultimately to get yourself talking about why you want to make the change.

Questions for Reflection

1. What decisions leave you stuck most often?

2. How does your ambivalence protect you from moving forward?

3. When is it okay to remain ambivalent?

Chapter 30

Embracing The Relationship Learning Curve

We have all seen people who look like naturals at whatever they are doing. Like many of you, I have watched the Olympics, and I have been so impressed by the abilities of the athletes from around the globe. It seems like they have always been able to skate with grace or glide with speed, but once I hear their full back stories, I am reminded of all the hard work and ongoing training athletes go through to get to that place of excellence in their sport.

Hearing stories about these Olympians reminds me of the learning curve that we all must embrace when we enter into and stay in marriage. Put simply, the learning curve requires tremendous effort to get started into a new activity. Once we begin, it will take time to develop and grow to a place where we will feel confident in our ability to maintain what we have learned. The relationship expert Harville Hendrix said, "The learning curve in relationships must be embraced." I interpret that to mean that we are not naturals at every dynamic of married life, particularly when we first start down that road. So, we must exert significant effort to grow in order to appear "natural" in our relationships. Each person will bring different areas of strengths and weaknesses to the table. Recognizing your strengths and weaknesses, and then doing something about them, will help develop a committed marriage bond. Over time, with focused hard work, we can all enjoy the fruits of embracing the learning curve. It is also important to remember that there will be seasons in your marriage when a new learning curve shows up. Here are 5 places you can expect that to happen.

- The start of your marriage
- The birth of a child
- The change of a job
- The death of a loved love
- The kids leaving home for college

Fortunately for you, there are also some simple steps you can take when starting on the learning curve.

1. Recognize that you are entering the learning curve.
2. Move into the learning curve by identifying what you need to learn.
3. Expect setbacks and challenges, even after you've reached mastery.
4. Ask for help and get guidance. Those who get to mastery never do it alone.
5. Practice over and over, and look for immediate feedback when possible.

So, maybe your marriage is not where you want it to be. What would be different if you embraced the learning curve?

I recently listened to a great interview of Karen Cheng, who learned to dance in 100 days. Could your marriage be completely different in 100 days? Check out Karen's interview and dance video for inspiration.

Questions for Reflection

1. What strengths do you bring into your marriage?

2. What weaknesses do you bring into your marriage?

3. How do both your strengths and weaknesses impact your marriage?

Chapter 31

Moving Towards Hope

"You don't need coping skills, you need hoping skills, impossible is nothing for God" - Dr. Margaret Nagib

This is a quote I heard from Dr. Margaret Nagib, who led a workshop during the 2013 American Association of Christian Counselors conference. This was one of those paradigm (belief) changing workshops. How often have we all been caught just trying to find ways to get by, and not looking for ways to thrive?

So what is hope? It is the overall perception that a goal can be met. There are two primary components of hope. The first is agency thoughts, which represent the drive to get something done. The second is a pathway to achievement, seeing that there are multiple ways to get something done. The people that feel the most accomplished and fulfilled out of life are not the most intelligent, but rather the ones that know that they can get it done. In other words, they remain hopeful.

Why pursue hope? It can lead to; physical, mental, and emotional health, a meaningful life, academic success, improved athletic performance, patience, and gratitude, to name a few.

Dr. Nagib also introduced a simple formula for pursuing big dreams.

Hoping = Big Dreams and Coping = Little Dreams

If you are ready to start developing hope, consider a dream journal. Write out 100 dreams. To help you get started, think about; travel, financial, education, hobbies, kids, family, legacy, and professional dreams.

As Christians, we know that our ultimate hope is in the Lord, but that does not mean we cannot have additional hopes and dreams.

Hoping Means
Trusting Him with everything you got
Choosing His peace when things don't make sense
Phil. 4:7

Breaking off the lies and bad partnerships
Hope does not disappoint us Rom. 5:5.

Questions for Reflection

1. What are you hopeful about?

2. What drives you to get something done?

3. What pathways are available to accomplish your hopes?

Relationships

Chapter 32

Creating Financial Success In Your Marriage

Getting on the same page: What would financial success look like in your marriage?

The absence of fighting about money?
Having an emergency fund?
Buying a home?
Purchasing a second home?
Writing a big check to charity?
Something else?

Chances are that you and your spouse are in the same chapter of the book, but perhaps not on the same page about what it means to be financially successful. What are you doing to get there? Too often, I have seen couples who have either stopped talking about money or fight non-stop about money. Either way, this disconnect usually ends up creating a huge wedge in their relationship. That's because both people typically have their own individual thoughts on what financial success looks like. Instead of working

135

together to create a vision for their family, they are locked in a battle over money.

Here are 4 simple steps toward defining what financial success would look like in your marriage.

1. **Realize** this is not about winning a battle, but rather creating a life together.

2. **Accept** that you and your partner are not going to see eye-to-eye on everything.

3. **Allow** the definition of financial success to evolve as your family grows and changes.

4. **Ask** the question meaningfully and intentionally, "What would financial success look like for *us*?"

An infinite number of discussions about money will arise during the course of your marriage, but the first step is to work toward realizing that you are in this *together*. When two people work together and not against one another, they create a profitable and fulfilling financial life as a joint unit. At the end of the day, it is not about accumulating the most money, but rather enjoying the marriage and family that you build together. So, take some time to slow down and get on the same page.

Questions for Reflection

1. What does financial success look like for your spouse?
2. How often do you take time to ask about your spouse's dreams and aspirations?
3. What can you do to become more comfortable with a fluid definition of financial success?

Stop Fighting & Start Talking

Chapter 33

Explicit and Implicit Money Lessons From Your Family

Have you ever considered how your family implicitly and explicitly taught you many different lessons about money? Today, I would like to share with you a couple of ways to think about that question.

1. **During Childhood** - Did your parents all too happily buy you whatever you wanted whenever you wanted? If so, why? Was it to please you and make up for a lack of something they did not have as a child? Or maybe your parents were experiencing guilt about not spending enough time with you and tried to cover that guilt with gifts? Maybe the opposite was the case, and your parents would not buy you anything you wanted. Why is that? Perhaps they were trying to teach you responsibility and that relationships are more important than stuff? It could have also been that they just did not have that kind of disposable

139

income. Whatever the reason, that surely left you with a certain feeling. Take a moment to reflect on what feelings you experienced.Understanding what happened with money during your childhood can help you to better appreciate your money values as an adult. Money values are simply the beliefs you have about the way money should be used and what it means. Often, we are unaware of our money values, and that is why we stay in money ruts.

2. **Family Money Rules** - Every family has a money paradigm, which is a way that they think about finances. It influences simple things like from when to go out to eat and what clothes to buy, to the types of vacations you take, to thinking about whether you should save for the future. How did your family arrive at these money decisions? What priorities did they set with the money they had? Perhaps there were no priorities and that was the money rule of your house. Now, take some time to brainstorm your family's money rules. How do they influence the way you interact with money now? Which of the rules needs to be changed and why? One of my family money rules that I learned from my Dad was to research like crazy before buying a big-ticket item. I got the

impression we didn't have to go for the cheapest things, but we wanted to find something that was going to last. While I will admit I don't do loads of research before I make similar purchases now, I do think about long-term value instead of just getting something cheap.

Questions for Reflection

1. What explicit money rules did your parents teach you?

2. What implicit money rules did your parents teach you?

3. What rules are you trying to rewrite for your life now?

Chapter 34

Friendly Finances

What do our friends have to do with our finances? Much more than we realize, believe it nor not. While we are all well aware of "keeping up with the Jones [family]," do we really know how that idea is influencing us? Stop and take a minute to make a list of your last 10 major purchases (goods or services). Now, choose several of your closest friends and list the last 10 major things you remember *them* buying. Compare how many items overlap.

Having trouble coming up with ideas? Here are a few: school items or tuition, cars, homes, vacations, birthday gifts, anniversary gifts, financial planning services, accounting services... Still can't think of big things? Think about restaurants, gyms, hair stylists, and favorite stores. If you really want to get bold in your comparison, put down prices and frequency of purchases. This will really illuminate how similar your buying decisions are to your friends'.

When I did this exercise, one item that came up was a house. My wife and I bought a home recently, and it is remarkable how similar in size and price our home is to that of our friends, who recently purchased homes as well. Many times, using our friends' buying decisions can be a significant help, because they save us time and energy in researching a great product or service. In other cases, it can have a profoundly negative impact. For example, if you buy a home that is beyond your price point, but you do it anyway because you figure if your friends can make it happen, then surely you can too.

Why is it important for you to understand how your friends influence your money decisions? Because once you get it, then you have the power to change your situation. If you are like most of us, the way you spend money is not fully congruent with your values. Start making the changes you desire by first identifying what's holding you back.

Questions for Reflection

1. What decisions do you make that are similar to your friends?

2. What do you disagree with about how your friends use money?

3. What values do you communicate to friends about money? Intentionally and unintentionally?

Chapter 35

Making The Most of Your Marriage and Money

What are you doing to increase your effectiveness in your marriage and with money? Both of these areas require continuing effort to increase your level of satisfaction with either one. It is my belief that if you improve your marriage, your financial position will improve, and that if you improve your financial position, you will improve your marriage. Marriage and money issues are linked. They both require attention.

We too often see education as an expense and not an investment. Sure, you often have to give up some time and pay some money to learn, but what you learn in return should pay you back in spades. When you study and apply healthy marriage and money habits, over time, you build a deep resource pool to draw on when you face the challenging times. The best time to prepare for challenges is when there are none.

In no particular order, here are 5 of my favorite books that address either marriage or money topics.

1. The Five Love Languages by <u>Gary Chapman</u>. **Why you should read it** - to learn how your spouse receives love differently than you do and how to respond to them in a way so that they will feel loved.

2. Love Talk by <u>Drs. Les & Leslie Parrot</u>. **Why you should read it** - practical guidance on creating time and space to talk with your spouse.

3. Love and Respect by <u>Dr. Emerson Eggerichs</u>. **Why you should read it** - to understand the cycle that often leaves you in conflict.

4. The Millionaire Mind by <u>Thomas Stanley</u>. **Why you should read it** - to dispel many of the myths you may have about what it is like to be rich.

5. Smart Couples Finish Rich by <u>David Bach</u> **Why you should read it** - this is the most practical book on everything from getting

organized, to managing debt, to investing. Start here if you don't know where else to start as a couple.

When you take time to understand how your marriage and money can work together, then you not only impact your life, but the lives of many others. Let's face it, whether you love, hate, or are indifferent about money, it impacts your marriage. You might as well make the most of it and make it meaningful.

Questions for Reflection

1. What books have had the greatest influence on your marriage? Why?

2. What books have had the greatest influence on your finances? Why?

3. What is one area that would benefit you to know more about in your marriage or finances?

Chapter 36

Money Conflict? Getting On The Same Page.

I recently met with a financial planner who was feeling frustrated that his clients did not share the same perspective as he did. This conversation reminded me of the common experience I hear about in marriage when each spouse is on a different financial page then the other. This can be a really frustrating experience for both spouses.

Over time, and with skill, there is hope that two spouses can come together and start to make decisions together. It starts with empathetic listening. What does it mean to listen with empathy? It means that you put down your defensiveness and really seek to first understand where the other person is coming from. The question you should be asking yourself is "Why do they view things the way that they do?" In order to accomplish this, it is important to listen first, and then reflect back the feelings your spouse is communicating. The trick is that often when you fight about money, it looks like anger, but underneath that anger is another emotion. It may be one of fear, distrust, worry, or violation. When you can identify with your spouse's true feelings, it will lower their defenses and it will then create a unique opportunity to have a real and vulnerable conversation about your finances.

Questions for Reflection

1. What makes it easy to listen to your spouse?

2. What makes it difficult to listen to your spouse?

3. What would it be like to give up your foregone conclusions about your spouse's perspective?

Chapter 37

Why Conflicts Keep Repeating In Marriage

How often do you feel like you are having the same argument today that you had yesterday, and the year before, with your spouse? If your marriage is like many others, you get to a place where you can anticipate the argument before it comes. Often, as arguments start to repeat themselves, frustration settles in and you become entrenched in proving your point, which then prevents you from listening to what your partner is really saying.

Arguments in marriage are comprised of two components. The first part is the subject and sounds something like this - "You spend too much money, your never home on time, you are...."fill in the blank. During this part of the argument, there is an accusation that involves the use of "you" to point out what your partner has done or not done to offend you. In most marriages, this is where the couple tries to resolve the argument by trying to get their partner to change their behavior.

155

Yet the problem continues to come up. Why?

The source of the argument lies below the subject of the argument, in the emotions and feelings of your partner. In order to start overcoming the subject of the argument, it helps to understand the source of the argument. The source of the argument often involves either violated feelings or personal beliefs that have been challenged.

Steps to recognizing the source of the argument
1. Recognize that you are entering into an argument.
2. Take a deep breath.
3. Ask your partner what is important to them about whatever the subject of the argument is.
4. Ask why that is important to them and listen for the emotion or belief behind the response.
5. Validate the feeling or belief they have. This does not mean you agree, but it demonstrates that you understand.
6. Then ask them if you can share how you feel about the situation.

For example, a wife is continuously frustrated that her husband comes home late from work (subject of argument) and she is ready to get to the bottom of it, but instead of getting mad at him this time, she follows the six steps of recognizing the source of the argument. In this example, let's call the wife Pam and her husband Dave.

Step 1. Pam recognizes that she and Dave are about to get into an argument if she confronts him about coming home late once again.

Step 2. Pam takes a deep breath.

Step 3. Pam asks Dave, "What is so important to you about staying at work late"? Dave may respond with any number of different responses. But it may be something as simple as, "There is an upcoming promotion that I really want to get."

Step 4. Pam now knows what Dave is working towards, a promotion, and now is going to try and understand why the promotion is important to Dave (Pam should try not to infer her own meaning and really just focus on what Dave says.) Pam asks Dave, "Honey, why is this promotion important to you?" Again, Dave may give any number of responses. In this case, Dave says, "I really want the promotion so that we can afford to go on a family vacation this year." So in this case, the source of the argument is Dave's desire to take his family on vacation.

Step 5. Pam now realizes Dave is not trying to avoid the family, but rather he is trying to create an opportunity for the family to go on vacation together this year. Pam responds to Dave with validation, saying, "Honey, it sounds like it is important to you that we go on a family vacation together this year."

Step 6. Now that Pam has taken the time to understand what is important to Dave about staying at work (subject of argument), and she validated Dave for his desired outcome of a vacation (source of argument), Dave will likely be more receptive to hearing Pam. Pam can now share with Dave what is important to her about having him home on time and why that is important.

Let's be honest - we all know that conversations that are charged with differing emotions and beliefs will not follow a perfect sequence of six steps and then a happy ending. However, what I hope that you get from these steps is a framework for how to move through conversation and a desire to look for the source of the argument, so that you do not get stuck at the subject of the argument.

Questions for Reflection

1. How does having a process for an argument change your approach?

2. Which step is most difficult for you and why?

3. What will be different when you get to the source of the argument?

Chapter 38

Let Go Of Your Agenda And Get To Know Your Partner

I was recently venting to a friend about how busy I 've been lately and what a struggle it has been to connect with my wife on a daily basis.

We've all been there with our significant others; that moment when our impatience prevails, and we think (or even say),"I don't have time to listen right now, honey. Just tell me what I need to know before I have to head to my next meeting, kids' event, or whatever else requires my immediate attention." Over time, the frantic pace of life can cause a distant feeling in our marriages. If that distance is left unattended to for too long, it will most definitely lead to conflict.

So, how do we prevent conflict when we sense it on the horizon? For me, it boils down to making time to converse with my wife without an agenda. Too often, when we engage with our spouses, the dialogue ends up being about necessary details that keep life moving forward. Our son's baseball game. The dog's veterinary appointment. The car needing to go to the mechanic (definitely not dating fodder, so why should it dominate the discussion now?). Because of this, we miss the opportunity to inquire about how the other person is doing and feeling, which is vital to maintaining any meaningful relationship

Tips for Talking

- Share with your spouse that you want to hear *how* they are doing, not *what* they are doing.
- Find a quiet room in the house (no TV, no tablet, no children) and ask your spouse what he/she dreams about.
- Go for a walk with no direction or distance in mind. Allow the conversation to dictate your path.
- For something more romantic, take a bath together. Embrace intimacy.

When we stop and remember that we married our spouses to be in a lifelong relationship with them, and not just to get things done, we can take the time to move from the necessary exchange of information to the heart of connecting conversation: feelings, aspirations, and dreams.

Questions for Reflection

1. Why did you marry your spouse?

2. What have you come to appreciate most about them?

3. How do you respond when they act favorably?

Chapter 39

4 Quick Tips to Getting Over Your Money Arguments

Money arguments are a normal part of the marriage relationship, so it is important to have a framework for working through those arguments. Here are three simple tips to help you get through the money fights.

1. Encourage Fun and Reassurance. Identify ways that you can have fun together outside of the arguments you are having about money.

2. Be Giving and Loving. Develop an attitude of gratitude for the things your partner is doing right.

3. Shift Your Mentality from Poverty to Wealth. Identify the things that you do have (i.e. job, house, cars, each other, kids, etc.) instead of being focused on what you do not have.

Questions for Reflection

1. What material things do you have?

2. What relationships do you have in your life that are important to you?

3. What are three ways you can have fun together? Commit to not brining up money issues.

Chapter 40

Not Just Money: Fears, Feelings, And The Pressures Of Marriage

Why is it that most married couples seem to fight about money over and over again, year after year? Because money is more than just a means of buying the things we need in life. Money represents, and is often used to express, our feelings. Those feelings can develop into different fears and pressures within our relationships, which can then cause us to do things with money that are actually detrimental to the partnership. When couples are in the midst of a heated debate about money, they often don't think about looking beyond the superficial argument at hand to recognize the actual feelings, fears, and pressures that exist.

To help illustrate what I'm talking about, let's look at the case of a typical American family. Bob and Sally have been married for nine years. They have two children, Max and Suzy. Since getting married, they have both enjoyed careers that have gradually placed them into roles that require more and more responsibility. However, with the ever-increasing demands of work and home life, both Bob and Sally have recently felt like the initial chemistry they once shared has worn off, and they are starting to fight about money more frequently.

Bob and Sally's typical argument goes something like this:

Bob: *Here we go again. You always have a problem when I spend money hanging out with the guys.*

Sally: *I am not mad. I just wish you'd prefer to spend your free time at home with our family, that's all.*

Bob: *Well, if you would let me hang out with my buddies from time to time, then I would be more excited about coming home. I couldn't tell you the last time I had a guys' night.*

Sally: *Why do you say that? I just think we need to be saving money right now. You know as well as I do how tight things are around here.*

Bob: When will things ever not be tight? You know I am working my butt off with no promotion in sight. I have to get away from the office and our home every now and then or I will go crazy.

You get the idea. Now, Bob and Sally think that if they could just learn how to talk to each other in a respectful, diplomatic manner, then they wouldn't have these arguments. But even if they did increase their ability to openly share their feelings without conflict, they still need to go beyond what is literally being said and understand the values and metaphors that are being communicated. That is, why are Bob and Sally *really* fighting?

First, let's take a look at their financial picture.
1. Their mortgage costs 20% of their income (very reasonable level.)
2. They have four months of expenses saved (healthy level.)
3. They both regularly contribute to their respective companies' retirement funds.

Based on that, it seems like things are not actually all that bad for Bob and Sally from a financial perspective. So, the problem isn't about "things being tight," as they have plenty of resources to carry them through a tough season. It's also not the surface-level issue of Bob wanting to spend time with his friends. What, then, is really happening?

In short, Bob and Sally's feelings, fears, and pressures about their relationship have not been openly addressed, simply because they have been "too busy" focusing on work and raising their kids.

The truth is that Bob is overwhelmed in his IT role. His company continues to hire younger employees who are outperforming him. This has caused Bob to feel uncertain about his future at the company. Because of this uncertainty, Bob's self-confidence and sense of pride are being challenged. Sally, meanwhile, is feeling pressure because she grew up in a family where there was never enough money, and she subconsciously believes that that the more money in the bank, the better.

Sound familiar?

Who wants to waste time fighting about money? Not me (or you, I presume.) Yet, at one point or another during our marriages, we will in fact face some dispute over money; perhaps multiple disputes. But the reality is that, when we fight about finances, the conflict tends to be about a lot more than what's on the surface.

What is happening to Bob and Sally? For them, the argument over money was rooted in the fact that Bob was feeling fearful about his future job stability, and Sally was still holding on to the pain of not having enough to go around as a child. Bob wants to get away every once in a while to forget his troubles, but Sally doesn't want the family to spend any discretionary money because she'd rather see it all go into their bank account.

If you are like Bob and Sally and find yourself butting heads with your partner like this, there is hope: you can indeed work through your arguments. You just might need to consider a new approach.

Try these five actions to help you move away from the topic of money and toward the feelings, fears, and pressures behind the money argument.

171

1. Remain open-minded and curious about why your spouse is bringing up the issue. Remember that there are two ways to respond: logically or emotionally. The reality is that most of us respond with a bit of both, so we want to acknowledge both the logical and emotional components of our partner's perspective.

2. **Ask**, "When you bring up _____ about money, what do you want me to know?" This will help you to see where your partner is coming from and hopefully give you a fresh perspective on what they are really communicating.

3. **Ask**, "Why is _____ about money important to you?" This is important because most of us haven't ever thought as much about why something is important to us. We just know that it is.

4. **Ask,** "What pressures and fears are you experiencing in life right now that I don't know about?" This will help you reconnect with your partner when life has gotten busy.

5. **Communicate with your spouse,** "When you

bring up _____ about money, it makes
me feel _____.,which causes me to
_____." This will help you to
connect the dots for your partner about why you
are responding the way that you are.

At the end of the day, moving beyond your money
arguments requires a growing amount of empathy
and a desire to truly know your partner for all
their strengths and limitations. When the
inevitable money arguments come up, slow down
and take your time to really understand where
your partner is coming from, and don't just
presume that you know because of past
experience.

Questions for Reflection

1. What part of Bob and Sally's story do you connect with and why?

2. What would happen if you no longer fought about your money differences?

3. How does having different frameworks for working through arguments help?

Chapter 41

How Specialization Gets Us In Trouble

By choosing one path in life, we give up many others. This is the nature of decision-making. Ultimately, as we pursue our career paths, many of us become more and more specialized in certain industries and specific jobs within our respective fields. What does specialization allow us to do? The specialist can see problems that many other people could never even dream of seeing. Moreover, they are often the experts on how to solve them. Sounds perfect, right? The issue, however, is that, as we specialize, we often start to lose perspective on many other dynamics of life.

So often in our marriages, we try to use our professionally developed skills to run our families. But what if your specialty at work does not support the emotional health of your family? Let's say you are an accountant and at work, it requires precision and accuracy, with all the details, but when you get home, what happens when you can no longer control all the details? It may be time for consultation on how to become more flexible in your family life.

As we pursue our professional specialization, we tend to get more and more comfortable at work, but if we do not also put significant effort into building and maintaining our family, we can lose perspective on how to be with and enjoy them.

Specialists also tend to have an ever-narrowing view of how to solve problems. Perhaps another example will help. After graduating high school, I became a professional fire fighter. My colleagues and I would often go to homes where people did not know where their water shut off was or where their breaker box was, and we would ask ourselves, "How do these people not know these really simple things about their own houses? We can see by their property that they are smart and successful in their careers. What's the deal?"

The reality is that the people who owned those homes spent more time building their careers then maintaining their houses. So what seemed like practical knowledge to a fire fighter was a bit distant or not important to the homeowner. Since moving on from fire fighting, I now have a greater understanding of this dilemma. As I have progressed through my adult life, earning several master's degrees and focusing on a career as a financial consultant, I find myself less interested and less able to care for the practical things around my family's home. I would rather have someone else come out to fix things that I normally would have taken the time to do myself.

Is specialization bad? No, not at all; on the contrary, it allows us to become more efficient at recognizing and solving many complex problems. The reality is that everyone is a specialist in some way, shape, or form, such as:

The stay-at-home parent - They know when the kids need to get up, go to school, turn in assignments, what groceries to buy, and the list goes on. It's not that the other parent isn't aware these things are happening; they just won't know them in the same detail.

The school teacher - Think about it: do you know how to assess if a third grader is making adequate progress through class, or how to teach high school algebra? I wouldn't know where to start.

The graphic artist - Definitely a specialist. They know how to create beautiful things for us to enjoy. They always seem to have a talent for picking just the right colors, fonts, images, etc. to make something look absolutely perfect.

The business person – Oh, there are too many types to list, but each business person develops a specific skill set that allows him or her to help support/run a business.

What we need to remember as specialists is that we develop a unique perspective on how the world works and how things get done. But we should not allow our focus on our specialty to stop us from examining how we function in our marriage and family life. The reality is that it takes a different skill set to build a flourishing family, and just as you have become an expert in your profession, it will take effort and continuous work to be an expert in your family. The outcome of that effort, however, can lead to you having a place that you love calling home.

Questions for Reflection

1. How does your specialization impact the way that you see the world?

2. How does your specialization negatively impact your family life?

3. How does your specialization positively impact your family life?

Chapter 42

Don't Shoot The Messenger

Making good financial decisions can be hard work. Most of us arrive in the adult world never having taken one class on personal finance. Sure, you saw your Mom use her credit card at the department store and your Dad go off to work every day. But what did you really learn about how to effectively manage personal finances?

Family life can be very demanding, and the basics of living often don't get covered in daily conversations. Heck, many of our parents never learned how to manage their personal finances, so can we fault them for not teaching us how to do the same?

Our families are the messengers of life lessons. We grow up watching our parents' every move. We are students of what they do and don't do. We notice the small things, like when Mom says she's a saver, but never seems to have money for the really big things. Or when Dad gruffly reflects,

"Another day, another dollar." These messages teach us to view money in a certain way. The family language of money often has to be decoded, and we must examine the money messages our parents give us. Unless we tackle our financial uncertainties, we can be left feeling stuck, frustrated, and scared about managing the financial resources we have.

Yet, in rare cases, there are those who feel financially secure. Yep, I said it: there are people out there who feel totally, unconditionally, 100% financially secure... but they are not who you think they are. They are not always the richest people in town - they are the people who have a good sense for what money can and cannot do for them in their life.

How did these people get to a place of financial security? It was not magic, I can assure you. They took the time to look at what they learned from their family, determined what was helpful, and then intentionally integrated that into their way of living. They also determined what negative views of money they had and let go of them. The financially secure identified the gaps in their knowledge of how to manage money, and then took time (and continue) to learn how to better manage the resources they have. Common learning experiences include reading books, attending classes, and finding trustworthy advisors to help teach them how to manage money and expectations well.

IMPORTANT LESSON: While learning to save, budget, and invest is important, the number one tip to financial security is to learn *how to manage your expectations*. It is the gap between where we are and where we expect we should be at any stage in life that is most likely to make us feel financially insecure.

Don't get upset with your parents because they did not teach you everything you need to know about money. Don't have an attitude with your wife because you are not on the same page about money. Chances are your spouse didn't get all the right money messages, either. There is a significant possibility that you and your wife share some financial views. Likewise, there is a strong possibility that you will also think differently on certain topics.

To address the similarities and differences in

money management approaches in your marriage, take time with your spouse to list out where you are on the same page and where you are different. When you identify those differences, realize that neither of you may be right and that there may be other options for managing that situation then what you have considered. This is where learning about personal finance together can introduce new ideas to your family. If you don't take the time to study personal finance, then all you will have to base your decisions on are the lessons from your own family, which won't always serve you well.

Questions for Reflection

1. What negative money lessons did your family pass along to you?

2. What positive money lessons did your family pass along to you?

3. What do you need to learn to move your life forward?

Chapter 43

Help I Married An Artist

The idea of the passionate, starving artist is an enigma in our culture. There is a long tradition of artists not wanting to share their work or get paid for it, as they fear it will cheapen their work.

So, how do you live with "the artist?" They hold a unique and distinct worldview around money. You try to talk to them logically, but they just won't change. What are you to do? Separate or divorce? How about taking another path instead?

Meet your artist at the emotional level of their art. This is probably going to be a stretch for you; you married your artist for their passion and authentic style. It is what you fell in love with because it was so different from your own sense of self. But now you have to come to terms with the fact that they are not going to be a financially contributing member of the family. You think in accounting terms. The accounts are not balanced. You say to yourself, "I work all day, and all they do is create." Sure, sometimes it takes time for the artist to hit their stride; deny their art, and they decree that they will die. This is when you should ask your spouse some open-ended questions to see if you can better understand where they are coming from and what might motivate them to change.

1. Honey, what originally drew you to your art?

2. What motivates you to continue to create new art?

3. What does your art represent to you?

4. What message are you trying to communicate to the world?

5. What would the world be like if they never heard your message?

6. What ways would you like to get your message out that would be authentic for you?

The old saying is, "Do what you love, and the money will follow." Well, that is a half truth. You do need to pursue what you love, but the money often does not start coming until you ask for it. For many artists, they want to know that their art is going to serve a greater purpose before they start focusing on making a living from it. Encourage your artist to see their work in a different light. Let them know they can still care deeply about their art and change the world without being a "sell out." Once they are committed to seeing how their art can be a legitimate contribution, then it is time to figure out ways to generate income.

* Small note artists, pastors, counselors, social workers, and doctors often have similar money rejecting scripts about accepting money for their services.

Questions for Reflection

1. What draws your spouse to their passion?

2. What did you learn about your spouse's passion?

3. What support does your spouse need to move their art to a profitable venture?

Chapter 44

Creating Money Harmony, Is it Possible?

Money fights in marriage are so common that we are often left to wonder if couples can ever experience "money harmony." I recently had the chance to ponder that issue when I interviewed Olivia Mellan, who is a trained psychotherapist, and has dedicated her career to helping couples develop money harmony in their relationship (and to helping individuals move towards money harmony as well.) Not only has Olivia worked with couples to overcome their biggest money fights, but she has also coached and spoken to countless personal finance professionals to help them better engage their clients in making great financial decisions. (Since 1996, she has written a monthly column in Investment Advisor magazine–www.ThinkAdvisor.com)

When I asked Olivia why couples fight about money in a marriage, she promptly responded that it all boils down to different priorities. Over the years, Olivia has identified a handful of ways that couples become polarized over money, including:

- *Saver vs. Spender* – The saver seeks to put away as much money as possible, while the spender sees a bright shiny object and buys it immediately.
- *Worrier vs. Avoider* – The worrier always has money on their mind and they're afraid of what is to come, while the avoider would rather not think about money at all.
- *Money Monk vs. Money Amasser* – The money monk sees no value in accumulating money, while the money amasser can't imagine not accumulating as much money as possible.
- *Planner vs. Dreamer* – The planner wants practical and realistic steps to accomplishing goals, while the dreamer knows what they want, but has no idea how to get there.
- *Risk Taker vs. Risk Avoider* – The risk taker is not afraid of losing some money in the pursuit of getting a big return, while the risk avoider doesn't want to lose a dollar in the process of saving.
- *Money Merger vs. Money Separatist* – The money merger sees the family finances as all going into one bucket, while the

money Separatist wants a mine, theirs, and ours bank account (some prefer completely separate money – others want some separate money.)

Olivia went on to share that if couples do not start out with opposing views on money, then in time, they will start to polarize over the use and role of money in their relationships. In couples with empathy and positive communication skills, these differences can complement and balance each other well, which allows the couple to create a balanced view and approach to managing household resources. The challenge comes when each person in the relationship does not identify the role they are playing in that partnership, and then they are unable to see the other person's perspective.

To help couples move through their repeating money fights, Olivia offered two great pieces of advice.

1. Gain Insight – Have a conversation/dialogue with money as if it were a person. Tell it how you feel about it and what role it plays in your life. Have it respond to what you write – a

dialogue, back and forth. Then, take time to share those thoughts with your spouse. Then have these internal voices: Mom, Dad, other strong influences, and God/Higher Power/your voice of inner wisdom comment on the dialogue with money.

2. Behavioral - Practice the non-habitual by walking in the other person's shoes. Some simple examples would be that if you buy the groceries, let your spouse do that. If you pay the bills, let your spouse do that. If you plan the investments, let your spouse do that. If you're the saver, spend money on some immediate pleasure purchase for you or your partner. If you're the spender, put money in savings or add to your investments.

3. Practice communicating with empathy and respect in weekly, regular money talks. Agree on a time frame for short, medium, and long term goals. Then generate individual lists on your own, several times, to see which goals come up again and again. Then merge some of the items on your list so that you feel more aligned in your money and life goals.

It's going to take work to move toward money

harmony in your marriage, but with some time and continuous effort, you can make it a reality.

Questions for Reflection

1. What areas of polarization do you align with?

2. What areas of polarization does your spouse line up on?

3. How do your polarizations help and hinder your marriage?

Thoughts and Logic

Chapter 45

Creating Vision, Just like A Polaroid Photo

Have you ever wondered why it is so hard to clearly develop your vision for the future?

There are many moving pieces to developing your vision for the future. It can be confusing to determine which pieces should take priority. I was recently reflecting on this issue myself and thought about it this way. Clarifying your values is like taking a Polaroid photo when you take the picture, you hope that you got everyone smiling and in the right pose. The picture comes out of the camera and you shake it for clarity. Then, after a few minutes, you realize you didn't quite get the photo you hoped for, so you start over. You get everyone lined up again, take another photo, shake it, nope, still not a good enough photo. One more time, you get everyone lined up, take the photo, shake it, and realize nope, still not a great photo. But by now you and everyone else are frustrated and ready to just get on with the activity of the day, so you live with the photo that you have taken.

This can also be how you develop your vision. You get everything lined up again, take a snap shot, shake it, realize it is not perfect, and keep on going, knowing that in time you can start the process again. We don't often get the right picture on the first try and it takes effort to get the final shot we want.

In this modern day of digital technology with instant feedback, we expect the rest of our life to work that way. We take a digital photo and we instantly know whether we are happy with it or if we need to take another photo. But in our everyday life, we seldom get that quick of feedback. Sometimes it takes days, weeks, months, or years before we can become really clear about where we are headed.

So take your time, take multiple shots at it, and realize that when you get frustrated, you can take another shot at your vision later. Allow your vision to develop over time. It will evolve as you get more information.

Questions for Reflection

1. What vision do you need to take another shot at?

2. What is the farthest out time period that you can think about?

3. What vision is developing right before your eyes?

Chapter 46

How Automatic Responses Get Us in Trouble

Recently, while I was at the YMCA, I was introduced to a woman by a friend of mine. During the introduction, I was told that she has a child that is autistic. In a moment without thought, I said "Oh, nice," to which the woman promptly said "No, it isn't." I felt terrible. What would normally be an innocent response left egg on my face. This interaction happened because of an automatic response I have when I am introduced to someone that has a child. Much like an auto responder on email, my brain knows that when someone is being introduced to me and they have a child, it is typically polite to say something to the effect of "Oh, nice." However, in this case, my auto response created an awkward moment.

This same thing happens all the time in our marriage. Our brain works on rules. The rules lead to automatic responses, which make everyday situations easier to navigate. In many situations, this works great, but there are times when our automatic responses fail us in our marriage, especially in the area of household finances.

When your spouse says we need to save more, buy the kids clothes, take a vacation, etc., your automatic response is...

Each of these statements are vague enough that they could mean any number of different things. So the goal becomes not just to automatically respond, but to ask for more clarification. Otherwise, your automatic response may lead to hurt feelings.

Questions for Reflection

1. What automatic thoughts get you in trouble?

2. What can you do to slow down your response?

3. What topics get your quickest response and why?

Chapter 47

Trust is A Key Ingredient to Financial Success

Why don't you feel like you are moving towards financial success?

Could it be that you don't trust the very elements that will help create financial success?

When I talk with people about building towards financial success, they tell me some of the most interesting stories about why they can't, won't, or haven't built financial success.

Here is a short list of what I have heard...
I don't trust the stock market - people lose a lot of money there.
I don't trust the real estate market - look at how housing prices fell.
I don't trust the economy, it is not predictable.
I don't trust my spouse, they are always...
I don't trust myself - every time I get some money saved, an "emergency" comes up.
I don't trust the government, those

Democrats/Republicans are the reason we are in the mess we are in.

I don't trust the international stock market, it is too risky.

When you walk around effectively saying I don't trust xyz, then it makes it hard to use that as a tool to build towards financial success. This is why I encourage people, when I work with them, to evaluate what they don't trust. Once they identify what they don't trust, then we can find ways to work on building trust.

When you understand how investing, the government, the economy, or the international markets really work, not just how you have heard about how they work, you can start to see that in fact, we are in a great position to build towards financial success.

When it comes to you and your spouse, sure you have made some bad marriage and money decisions. But you have the power to learn from those bad decisions. It can start with rebuilding trust in your relationship through having honest communication about your feelings.

The Lesson: The things you don't understand or misunderstand make it hard to trust. Learn to understand how the financial markets really work and how you and your spouse really relate, and then you will be on the path to trusting the tools that will build financial success.

Questions for Reflection

1. What is hard for you to trust about the economy?

2. What is hard for you to trust about your personal relationships?

3. What is hard for you to trust about yourself?

Chapter 48

How Money Sayings Get Us In Trouble

Money is one of those topics we love and hate to talk about. Most of us desire to have more of it, even if some of us tell others that we don't. Yet no matter what you believe about money, you probably have a saying about money that represents the way that you feel. Yet it is our very sayings about money that may be what limits us from developing a healthy relationship with money.

Here is a short list of sayings about money. How can these sayings mislead you?

- Money can't buy happiness
- Money is the root of all evil
- A penny saved is a penny earned
- Money makes the world go 'round
- Save your pennies for a rainy day
- Mo' Money, Mo' Problems
- A fool and his money are soon parted
- You can't take it with you

- Render unto Caesar
- A penny for your thoughts
- Money can't you me love
- Putting your money where your mouth is
- Dollar wise and penny foolish
- Spending money like a drunken sailor

I don't know about you, but after reading over this list of money sayings several times, I feel confused. What am I supposed to believe about money? This is the challenge when we rely on a saying or two about a topic that has a profound impact and influence over our life. The reality is that many of these sayings have grown out of a personal observation or experience, but without understanding the context of the saying, it may be misapplied in application to our life. Too often, the saying we have become familiar with has been adapted and with some parts dropped intentionally so that the saying makes sense for the context in which the message is being delivered. This is why we should not just accept a money saying at face value, but rather take time to question the origin and meaning of the saying.

Let's just take one of these sayings and understand the possible implications.

3 Problems/Challenges with "Money is the root of all evil."

This is a Biblical reference to Paul's letter to Timothy found in 1 Timothy 6:10. The actual verse reads v.10 *For the love of* money is a root of all kinds of evils. It is through this craving that some have wandered away from the faith and pierced themselves with many pangs.

1. Notice the verse includes the word love, which gives a completely different meaning to the sentence. Then in the second sentence Paul expresses his real concern, when some people have loved money, they have wandered from faith and pierced themselves with many pangs.

2. If you believe money is the root of all evil, no wonder you would not trust the rich, because they are the ones with loads of money. Or perhaps you believe they are rich because they love money and so then they are evil.

3. When you take a Biblical verse in isolation, then you miss the broader context of what the

Bible says about a given subject. To counter balance any ideas that money might be evil, consider the parable of the talents in Matthew 25: 14-30, where the first two servants took their given talents (equivalent to money) and doubled them. The last servant hid his and returned what was given to him. The first two servants were told well done good and faithful servant, where as the last servant was called a wicked and slothful servant.

Ultimately, the Bible references the management and use of money and resources over 2,000 times. Management of financial resources is a subject that creates many challenges because there are significant implications for how we view and use money.

The first step to understanding the role of money in our life is to decide what model or view of money we are going to take. Then we can set out on a journey to continually learn how to apply that model to the best of our understanding.

Questions for Reflection

1. What are your favorite financial sayings?

2. What are your spouse's favorite financial sayings?

3. What financial sayings do you deny? Why?

Chapter 49

Where Did All The Money Go?

Do you ever wake up at the end of the month and wonder where all the money went? Perhaps this is something you ask your spouse. Many couples are baffled because they honestly believe they do not spend that much. Sure, a little bit goes here and a little bit goes there, but that can't possibly all add up to the family paycheck - or does it? Getting a grip on how money flows through your life can help you start setting priorities for where and when you want the money to move.

There are three different types of expenses in life.

Fixed Expenses - Most of us feel like so many of our expenses are fixed, and we could not lower them or reduce them if we wanted to. But the reality is that most of our "fixed" expenses are actually semi-fixed, which I explain below. A fixed expense is the amount of money you need to sustain basic life: putting a roof over your head, food in your belly, and clothes on your back.

While it is not desirable to live at the minimum, it does take a basic level of income to sustain life, and depending on where you live in the world, that number varies.

Semi-Fixed Expenses - This is where our socioeconomic level really starts to fool us into thinking that our costs are fixed. Whatever part of town we live in starts to dictate our standard of living. This happens in part because we are social creatures, and while we pride ourselves on individuality, we often end up reflecting the values of the community around us. At whatever socioeconomic level you live, there is an implied minimum standard of living. When you take time to recognize how that standard is at work in your life, then you can start to make decisions about how you want to spend your money.

For example, when you move into a new neighborhood, you will intuitively be aware of the types of cars people drive, yard maintenance they keep, birthday parties they have for their kids, vacations they take, restaurants where they eat, career choices they make, and the list goes on. All of this information informs, at a subconscious level, the decisions each family makes with their money. (Think of the old adage "keeping up with the Joneses.")

Variable Expenses - This category reflects the differences in how each family allocates money toward their semi-fixed expenses. Some families love going out to eat together, while others value private school or want to win Garden of the Month. Ultimately, variable expenses represent the individual choices of families regarding how they want to live out their life.

As a couple, one of the most important things you can do to help advance your financial life together is to make intentional time for discussing family values. As a family better understands what it really values, they will start to make more intentional decisions about where the money goes.

Questions for Reflection

1. Which semi-fixed expenses do you feel are getting too much of your family's money (vacations, home upgrades, vehicles, etc.) and why?

2. What is one area of your life that is not getting the financial attention it needs (bills, debt, retirement, etc.)?

3. When we look back on our lives, what do we want to be able to say we did with our lives?

Chapter 50

Are You Living the Good Life And Don't Even Know It?

While cliché, it is so true that we get "wakeup calls" in life that tend to bring everything back into perspective. The wakeup call, by its very nature, crops up at the most peculiar times and in the most peculiar places. For me, it was when I found out I had melanoma (a form of skin cancer that can be deadly if undetected), or more recently, a Sunday morning, when I was sitting in church learning about the deep needs of Haiti. These wakeup calls summoned me to evaluate my own circumstances and ask, "Am I living the good life?" Upon reflection, I realized that, while I do not have everything I want, I do have everything I need. Learning to live in this realization is where deep contentment occurs. Too often, I hear people say that contentment leads to complacency, but what I have found is the opposite. When I am content, I am most motivated to continue to grow.

So, how do you know if you are living the good life? First, you must take the time to define for yourself what that actually means. The challenge (and temptation) is to base your definition of "the good life" on what others have or are doing, but that's not necessarily true and authentic to the way that you have been called to live. Sure, the perception of other people's circumstances will always be out there. But you must define for yourself what your good life looks like. What makes sense for you?

The process of defining the good life will look different for each person. For the highly structured and organized person, it may involve making a list and adding definitions. For the visual person, drawing may help them identify the characteristics of their "good life." Take some time to express in your own unique way what your good life looks like. Release the pressure of coming up with a definition quickly. If it needs to develop over a period of time, allow that to happen. The point is to be true to yourself through the entire process.

Once you have developed your idea of what it means to live the good life, take some time to think about your current situation. Where is there consistency in what you define as the good life and how you are living now? Where can you identify inconsistencies? As you reflect on these questions, consider that if there is 70 - 80% or more of your good life characteristics present in your life now, then you ARE living the good life. If your definition changes, that's okay. In fact, it's normal and healthy.

So, take a moment and look up to see that you are already living the good life. It is not "out there" somewhere. It is right under your nose.

Take this exercise one step further and include your spouse in this process. Remember, your definitions do not have to line up perfectly, but hopefully, there is overlap.

Questions for Reflection

1. How are you already living the good life?

2. How does your spouse define the good life?

3. What do you share in common and what is different?

Chapter 51

Your Greatest Financial Risk Is Not What You Think?

Risk is everywhere.

The potential for loss and its negative financial impact has allowed for the vast and complex world of the insurance industry to develop and thrive. As adults, we learn through many different lessons that we should fear economic loss, and that the best way to manage that risk is to make sure we have the proper insurances in place.

Often, our first introduction to insurance happens after getting a drivers license. Then, when we complete college and get our first job, we start to sort through health insurance. Life then continues on and, at some point, we start the process of building our family. We get married, buy a home, and have children, which bring on another host of

223

insurance policies to purchase: life, home owners', and disability.

Stay with me. I know talking about insurance and risk management is about as much fun as getting a root canal, but I promise I have a point.

Now that your family is growing, you start to think about college savings and retirement planning, and you realize that you not only need insurance, but you also need to be setting aside money for the future. So, you and your wife start to faithfully put money into your companies' 401K plans. You are no longer the kid learning to drive and hearing about insurance for the first time; you have a complex life with many different financial responsibilities.

Then one day, it happens: the financial risk you did not plan for, nor can you insure against or save enough money to prevent: divorce.

This news rocks your emotional, spiritual, and financial life. Everything changes. All the hard work of building, creating, and maintaining financial security evaporates and a myriad of questions about your financial security open up.

What can you do? We don't get married for financial support, do we? We (hopefully) get married because we love someone. Yet, over time, we come to trust our partner, and there is a financial element to the relationship. This is the very reason why we buy life insurance; we don't want to leave our spouse with an unreasonable financial burden in the event of our untimely death.

Creating marital stability and security at times can seem overwhelming, frustrating, and exhausting, but the effort is far worth it. While financial security should not be the determining factor in making a decision to stay married or get divorced, it is important to get help in really understanding the full cost of divorce from an emotional, spiritual, and financial perspective.

There is hope for restoration in marriage, even in the darkest of days. Consider working with a trained marriage and family therapist to help keep your marriage on the right track.

Questions for Reflection

1. What am I doing to strengthen my marriage?

2. Is my head in the sand about challenges in my marriage?

3. If there was one thing that I could start doing differently that would improve my marriage, what would it be?

Chapter 52

What is SMART Money Management?

Do you ever wonder what it takes to manage your personal finances well? This is a question I am constantly asking myself. So I created an acronym to help remind myself of the important aspects of managing finances.

SMART Money Management

Systems - How things get done
Measurement - Progress Made
Application - Getting it done
Results - Knowing what you want
Time - Periods to accomplish results

SMART Money Management is a way to remember the 5 key components of managing your personal finances. Each component of SMART is equally important. For those who are married, having SMART conversations can help keep the two of you on the same page.

Let's dig a little deeper in to what each component of SMART consists of.

Systems - This is how everything gets done in your financial life. From the simple things like buying groceries, to choosing how to pay for college, vacations, homes, and cars. It also includes how you pay your bills and pick investments. The important thing about systems is to recognize that we all have them, whether we have taken the time to set them up or not. In order to make better decisions, it is important to evaluate your systems and fine tune the ones that are not supporting your long term goals.

Measurement - The only way to know if you have made progress in your financial life is to have objective measures. In most cases, using a net worth statement is the most important tool to measure financial progress. The net worth statement is for your financial health, just as your weight is an indicator of your physical health. It does not tell you everything, but it gives you some important clues about how you are doing.

Application - Getting it done! If there is no application in money management, then you cannot expect to grow, but rather you should know that you will lose financial ground. It is important to actually take action on your plans. Often, this means taking many small steps that will lead to significant impact. You cannot wait until you have more money to take action. You must take action with what you have.

Results - Your desired results should be driving your systems, measurement and application. Results are all about knowing what you want to accomplish. If you do not take the time to decide on what you want, then you will never change what you are doing. Set some goals and start moving towards them. Your desired results will grow and change, but the important thing is to be working towards something.

Time - Without setting a period of time in which you want to get your results, you will never move towards the results you desire. When thinking about time, it is important to shoot for short term, intermediate, and long results.

*One special note. Don't let fear of failure stop you from defining the results you want and the time that you want to accomplish them in. You will make mistakes, but you will also have plenty of chances to adapt and set new desired results.

Questions for Reflection

1. What part of SMART money management was most helpful?

2. What part of SMART money management do you need to strengthen?

3. When will you improve your financial planning process?

Chapter 53

Moving Arguments To Resolution

Now, if you are still uncertain about how to bring conflict to resolution, I recommend using what I call the "Stop, Drop & Roll" method.

Stop - Recognize that you are entering a conflict. Either you are going to initiate it or your spouse is initiating with you. Remember, conflict does not always involve screaming and yelling; rather, it can include passive-aggressive behavior with subtleties that create tension but don't explode. Don't allow these conflicts to get buried deep down, because over time, it will lead to resentment. To better understand the impact of resentment on relationships, I recommend you look into the extensive work of Dr. John Gottman.

Drop - Drop your defenses and focus on what the other person is really upset about. There is a good chance that you may not fully recognize the source of their frustration. While your spouse may be bringing up a specific event or situation that has caused them to be upset, what you want to be listening for is the emotion behind the concern.*Example* – Recently, I had become annoyed that my wife would always ask, "Did you lock the car?" whenever we parked and walked toward a store. This made me feel like she thought I was not capable of remembering to lock the car. Silly, I know, but that is the way many arguments start: over something seemingly simple. Once I realized this question was frustrating me, and I asked my wife why she was always asking it, I learned something very interesting. She admitted that she regularly forgets to lock her car door. Her asking me if I locked the door had everything to do with her going through her own mental check list of leaving the car and nothing to do with me at all. Rather, she was just going through her own process to make sure the car was locked. No ill will was meant at all.

Roll - When you really understand where the other person is coming from, you must be ready to roll with the punches. Ultimately, your spouse will surprise you more often than not regarding the source of conflict and the way it makes them feel.

There you have it: Arguments are part of everyday life when living with someone. Next time something comes up, be ready to stop and recognize you are entering a conflict, drop your defenses, listen for the emotion behind the concern, and roll with the unexpected emotions and feelings of conflict.

Questions for Reflection

1. What does Stop look like for you?

2. What does Drop look like for you?

3. What does Roll look like for you?

Chapter 54

8 Tips for Picking a Great Financial Planner

Finding a great financial planner can be tough if you don't know what to look for. Here are eight important factors to consider when looking for, and choosing, a financial planner.

1. Do your personalities fit? You'll likely be meeting with them multiple times when getting started, and at least once a year after that, so it's important to know if you mesh.

2. Inquire about how the planner is compensated. If you cannot understand what they are explaining or they are hesitant to discuss their fees, that should signal a red flag.

3. Each planner is going to have a unique process, and it is important to inquire about theirs on the front end so that you know what to expect.

4. Ask the planner about some of the common products or services that they recommend at the

end of their planning process.

5. Find out who the planner is affiliated with, as this will give clues to the types of recommendations they are going to offer. Ultimately, there are three primary affiliations. A) Working under the name of an insurance companyB) Working under the name of a mutual fund companyC) Independent, non-affiliated (these planners typically have the most flexibility in product and service selection)

At the end of the day, each planner is going to have preferred products and services. This is not inherently good or bad; it is just something to keep in mind during your interactions.

6. Inquire if the planner has any particular areas of expertise. Have them explain what makes them an expert in that area.

7. Ask about any credentials the planner has and what they mean. If you really want to get into the nitty gritty of their qualifications, ask them about what it took to obtain those credentials. Credentials like the CFP® are widely recognized as a standard in excellence, but there are many

other credentials, such as ones created by the companies they work for, that are more promotional in nature than training-based.

8. Most importantly, have some ideas about what you want out of the financial planning process and be able to articulate them.

Selected Resources

Chapter 10 – Flourish by Dr. Catherine Hart Weber. www.Howtoflourish.com

Chapter 11 – Nurture Shock by Po Bronson & Ashley Merrymany. www.pobronson.com

Chapter 13 – Dr. Robert Emmons, The Science of Gratitude. http://gratitudepower.net/science.htm

Chapter 16 – Love Sense by Dr. Sue Johnson
http://www.drsuejohnson.com/books/love-sense/
And
Mind Over Money by Dr. Brad Klontz & Dr. Ted Klontz
http://www.yourmentalwealth.com

Chapter 17 – Book Yourself Solid by Michael Port. http://www.michaelport.com

Chapter 26 – Boundaries by Dr. Cloud and Dr. Townsend. http://www.boundariesbooks.com

Selected Resources Continued

<u>Chapter 30</u> – Dance in 100 Days (video), by Karen Cheng. https://giveit100.com/@karen

<u>Chapter 31</u> – Dr. Margaret Nagib. http://www.timberlineknolls.com/information/about/staff/christian-therapist-margaret-nagib

<u>Chapter 44</u> – Olivia Mellan – Money Harmony http://www.moneyharmony.com/index.html

Final Thoughts

The journey of marital and financial health is ongoing. It takes continual effort. At the end of your days I hope that you will be able to look back and say my life mattered to the people that matter most.

Invitation To Connect

The work of Ed Coambs and Marriage And Money Matters is ongoing and is always being updated.

Please Connect

www.MarriageAndMoneyMatters.com

www.Facebook.com/marriageandmoneymatters

Words of Appreciation, Insight Gained, and Life Change are welcome.

ed@marriageandmoneymatters.com

www.ingramcontent.com/pod-product-compliance
Lightning Source LLC
Chambersburg PA
CBHW051950090426
42741CB00008B/1338